Visions of the King

Timothy Raymond

TEACH Services, Inc.
PUBLISHING
www.TEACHServices.com • (800) 367-1844

All rights reserved. No part of this publication may be reproduced, distributed, or transmitted in any form or by any means, including photocopying, recording, or other electronic or mechanical methods, without the prior written permission of the publisher, except in the case of brief quotations embodied in critical reviews and certain other noncommercial uses permitted by copyright law. For permission requests, write to the publisher, TEACH Services, Inc., at the address below.

World rights reserved.

Unless otherwise noted, all scripture references are from the King James Version of the Holy Bible.

Copyright © 2020 Timothy Raymond
Copyright © 2020 TEACH Services, Inc.
ISBN-13: 978-1-4796-1228-4 (Paperback)
ISBN-13: 978-1-4796-1229-1 (ePub)
Library of Congress Control Number: 2020914424

Scripture taken from the New American Standard Bible®. Copyright © 1960, 1962, 1963, 1968, 1971, 1972, 1973, 1975, 1977, 1995 by The Lockman Foundation. Used by permission.

THE HOLY BIBLE, NEW INTERNATIONAL VERSION®, NIV® Copyright © 1973, 1978, 1984, 2011 by Biblica, Inc.® Used by permission. All rights reserved worldwide.

Scripture taken from the New King James Version®. Copyright © 1982 by Thomas Nelson. Used by permission. All rights reserved.

Scripture taken from the New Revised Standard Version Bible, copyright © 1989 the Division of Christian Education of the National Council of the Churches of Christ in the United States of America. Used by permission. All rights reserved.

Scripture quotations marked ASV are from the American Standard Version of the Holy Bible.

Published by

TEACH Services, Inc.
P U B L I S H I N G
www.TEACHServices.com • (800) 367-1844

Table of Contents

Preface v

Chapter 1: The Coming King... 7
Chapter 2: The King Becoming.. 18
Chapter 3: Prophesy Again... 28
Chapter 4: The Son of Man... 34
Chapter 5: The Stone Becomes a Mountain............................... 53
Daniel 2—Prayer of Praise... 68
Chapter 6: Prophesy About Kings....................................... 69
Chapter 7: Seated on a Cloud.. 75
Chapter 8: According to the Custom.................................... 82
Just a Thought #1—Anointed as King.................................... 90
Chapter 9: The Faithful and True Witness.............................. 93
Just a Thought #2—Pattern of Numbering............................... 103
Chapter 10: Michael Stands Up.. 106
Just a Thought #3—Earthly to Heavenly Type Antitype.................. 113
Chapter 11: The Midnight Cry... 115
Just a Thought #4—The Chiastic Structure of the Parable.............. 132
Chapter 12: The Latter Rain.. 134
Daniel 2—Prayer of Praise.. 158

Bibliography 159

Preface

The present is a time of overwhelming interest to all living. Rulers and statesmen, men who occupy positions of trust and authority, thinking men and women of all classes, have their attention fixed upon the events taking place around us. They are watching the strained, restless relations that exist among the nations. They observe the intensity that is taking possession of every earthly element, and they recognize that something great and decisive is about to take place--that the world is on the verge of a stupendous crisis.[1]

While the nations of this world scramble to address the coronavirus crisis and face the real possibility of world economic collapse; while the Pope gathers the leaders of this world to push his climate crisis and the indoctrination of the world's youth; while the storm of social change rages all around and even within the church; while everything that can be shaken is being shaken; while everyone's attention is transfixed on the events taking place on earth, this work is intended to call our attention to what's happening in heaven. Jesus is the hope of humanity. Christ is "all in all" (Eph. 1:23); He is the "beginning and the ending" (Rev. 1:8); He is the answer to all our crises. Last-day events are about Him. The things that transpire here on earth are a reaction to the position and work of our Lord in heaven. Cataclysmic events are unfolding on earth because something is happening with Jesus in heaven.

This work is not intended to be an exhaustive study of the topic. Rather, it is an introduction of the subject to stimulate thought, discussion, and further study. The Scriptures referenced to present the credibility of this thesis are explained in an attempt to verify the context and scriptural accuracy of their application, yet are not supposing to be a thorough exegesis of the text.

The greatest, most glorious event in the history of humanity is about to burst upon our dark planet. Jesus is getting ready to come. Are you ready for His coming? "Behold the Bridegroom cometh, go ye out to meet Him" (Matt. 25:6).

The King is coming!

---

[1] Ellen G. White, Education (Mountain View, CA: Pacific Press Publishing Association, 1952), p. 179.

Chapter 1

The Coming King

The Parousia; the second coming of Jesus Christ, the Lord of glory; the revelation of the Lamb; the coming of the Bridegroom; The appearing of the Messiah; the return of the King; the coming of "the messenger of the covenant" (Mal. 3:1); the "blessed hope, and the glorious appearing of the great God and our Saviour Jesus Christ" (Titus 2:13). These captivating phrases envision the most glorious, long-awaited, greatly anticipated event of all human history: when "the desire of all nations shall come" (Hag. 2:7) on "the great day of the LORD" (Zeph. 1:14)—the day that "the Son of Man shall come in His glory, and all the holy angels with him" (Matt. 25:31).

From the dawn of the first promise to Eve that her seed would crush the serpent's head (see Gen. 3:15) to the final announcement—"Surely I am coming quickly" (Rev. 22:20, NKJV)—the Scriptures have foretold the arrival of the Goel, our Kinsman Redeemer (see Ruth 4:14); the Christ event, when the Logos breaks through the terrestrial *ethos* to forever alter human *pathos*, fulfilling Christ's promise: "And if I go and prepare a place for you, and if I go and prepare a place for you, I will come again, and receive you unto myself; that where I am, there ye may be also" (John 14:2, 3); the return of the Author of life to the land of the shadow of death; the fulfillment of the heaven's pledge: "This same Jesus, which is taken up from you into heaven, shall so come in like manner as ye have seen him go into heaven" (Acts 1:11, KJV). Oh, don't you long for that day!?

In that magnificent day, we shall behold the face of Him who died to redeem us and bathe us in the glorious brightness of His radiant splendor. The living saints "shall all be changed, In a moment, in the twinkling of an eye … this corruptible must put on incorruption, and this mortal must put on immortality" (1 Cor. 15:51–53). Multitudes of those who sleep in the dust will awake (see Dan. 12:2) to look upon the face of Him who died to save them; the blessed hope of the ages who absorbed so much of their thoughts; the subject of their brightest expectations; and the object of their most cherished dreams.

> *In that magnificent day, we shall behold the face of Him who died to redeem us and bathe us in the glorious brightness of His radiant splendor.*

They went to sleep with the thought of Jesus in their hearts and His name on their lips. They will awaken at the trumpet call of His voice. The dark slumber of death will evaporate in the exhilarating brightness of His coming. The power of divine love will shatter the chains of death and hell and release those who, throughout their lives, loved His appearing. Death's sting will be vanquished, and tears of joy will replace the long, dark years of painful anguish. The blessed hope, a living reality. The promise of the ages ripping through the veil of time. The imminent becoming the present when "the Sun of righteousness arise[s] with healing in his wings" (Mal. 4:2).

Our lovely Jesus is the great Source of life from whom the healing streams of mercy, truth, and love flow out to lost humanity. "The light of the knowledge of the glory of God [shines] in the face Jesus" (2 Cor. 4:6). "To wit, that God was in Christ, reconciling the world unto himself" (5:19). The unveiling of God is the unfolding of "the treasures of wisdom and knowledge" (Col. 2:3) that were hidden in Christ from time and eternity but are now being manifest in His ministration for the salvation of lost humanity.

The day of the Lord—the time, space, and light of eternal truth—breaks through the veils of our darkened minds, preparing us to encounter the Self-existing Eternal One in all His glory. This day is rushing upon us. Are you ready? The time that has been graced to us at such great expense is all about preparing for this moment. Everything that happens in this life is part of the training necessary for our growth in Christ, to set us free from sin and prepare us to behold the face of Him who sits on throne (see Rev 6:16). He is faithful, and He will do it (see 1 Thess. 5:24).

However, there is more to the great controversy than our salvation. What appears to us to be a long delay is a necessary process that must unfold to answer the questions, disprove the accusations, and refute the objections raised by Lucifer's rebellion against his Maker. The Father must allow the process of rebellion to mature.

> All his acts were so clothed with mystery that it was difficult to disclose to the angels the true nature of his work. Until fully developed, it could not be made to appear the evil thing it was ...
>
> The true character of the usurper and his real object must be understood by all. He must have time to manifest himself by his wicked works. ...
>
> [Satan's] own work must condemn him. ...
>
> For the good of the entire universe through ceaseless ages, he must more fully develop his principles, that his charges against the divine government might be seen in their true light by all created beings, and that the justice and mercy of God and the immutability of His law might be forever placed beyond all question.[2]

What we recognize as the second coming of Christ is actually another plateau in the culmination of the process—the full development of the principles of both good and evil. It is the brightness of the light that exposes the mysterious deceit of the darkness. It is the rejection of that light and an embracing of the darkness that brings evil to its fullness. All gray areas will be exposed as rationalizations. All doubt and discontent will be made visible as excuses to justify sin and unbelief.

Then every intelligent being must and will choose for themselves which principles will govern their thoughts and actions; to which master will they pledge allegiance; to which kingdom they will become subject. Will the sacred law be inscribed on their hearts and minds, or will they remain lawless in rebellion to God? These choices result in living

---
[2]Ellen G. White, Patriarchs and Prophets (Washington, DC: Review and Herald Publishing Association, 1890), pp. 41, 42.

demonstrations of the principles of their respective kingdoms, reflecting the character and essence of their prince. Irrefutable evidence before the court of the universe removes the cloak of mystery surrounding the deceiver and exonerates the God of the universe from his fallacious accusations.

Jesus described this process in the parable of the wheat and tares:

> The kingdom of heaven is likened unto a man which sowed good seed in his field: But while men slept, his enemy came and sowed tares among the wheat, and went his way. But when the blade was sprung up, and brought forth fruit, then appeared the tares also. So the servants of the householder came and said unto him, Sir, didst not thou sow good seed in thy field? from whence then hath it tares? He said unto them, An enemy hath done this. The servants said unto him, Wilt thou then that we go and gather them up? But He said, Nay; lest while ye gather up the tares, ye root up also the wheat with them. Let both grow [together] until the harvest: and in the time of the harvest I will say to the reapers, Gather ye together first the tares, and bind them in bundles to burn them: but gather the wheat into my barn. (Matthew 13:24–30)

The disciples asked Jesus for an explanation, so He provided one:

> He that soweth the good seed is the Son of man; The field is the world; the good seed are the children of the kingdom; but the tares are the children of the wicked one; The enemy that sowed them is the devil; the harvest is the end of the world; and the reapers are angels. As therefore the tares are gathered and burned in the fire; so shall it be in the end of this world. The Son of man shall send forth his angels, and they shall gather out of his kingdom all things that offend, and them which do iniquity; And shall cast them into a furnace of fire: there shall be wailing and gnashing of teeth. Then shall the righteous shine forth as the sun in the kingdom of their Father. Who hath ears to hear, let him hear. (Matthew 13:37–43)

In the parable, the field is the world. There are only two groups, but they are not easily distinguished. The tares and wheat look a lot alike and are intertwined at the roots. The Master's concern for the wheat causes Him to wait for the maturing process to clearly reveal which is wheat and which is tares.

The harvest is the end of the world. What brings the plants to maturity are the sunshine and rain. This subtle truth is profound. The wheat cooperates in the process of maturing by receiving the sunlight of God's Word and the gift of the Holy Spirit, the early and latter rains. Those who receive it are described as the righteous who "shine forth as the sun" (v. 43). They come to reflect the character of their Father. The tares enjoy the gifts of time and opportunity granted but exploit them to iniquity. They grow to become "children of the wicked one" (v. 38) and reflect the character of the devil. The process brings both groups to maturity or completeness, then comes the harvest at "the end of the world" (v. 39). The Holy Spirit, speaking through Peter, proclaimed the same truth:

> Repent ye therefore, and be converted, that your sins may be blotted out, when the times of refreshing shall come from the presence of the Lord; And he shall send Jesus Christ, which before was preached unto you: Whom the heaven must receive until the times of restitution of all things, which God hath spoken by the mouth of all his holy prophets since the world began. (Acts 3:19–21)

Jesus must remain in heaven "until the time comes for God to restore everything" (NIV). In this statement, the restoration of all things is synonymous with the blotting out of sins and "the times of refreshing" that "shall come from the presence of the Lord." The times of refreshing—the outpouring of the Holy Spirit—brings the restoration of all things. Then, and not until then, "He may send Jesus Christ."

This bringing to maturity the revelation of the character of Christ in His saints is written of in many places. Paul wrote that the "earnest expectation of the creation waits for the revealing of the sons of God" (Rom. 8:19, NKJV). Peter wrote of the "salvation ready to be revealed in the last time" (1 Pet. 1:5). John implored us, "Beloved, now are we the children of God; and it has not yet been revealed what we shall be, but we know that when He is revealed, we shall be like Him, for we

> *These scriptures, along with many more, establish the truth that before we behold the revelation of Christ in the sky, there must be a revelation of Him in the lives of His people.*

shall see Him as He is. And everyone who has this hope in Him purifies himself, just as He is pure" (1 John 3:2, 3, NKJV).

These scriptures, along with many more, establish the truth that before we behold the revelation of Christ in the sky, there must be a revelation of Him in the lives of His people. "Christ is waiting with longing desire for the manifestation of Himself in His church. When the character of Christ shall be perfectly reproduced in His people, then He will come to claim them as His own."[3] How else could a dying world know that the option of salvation is available to them unless they see a living demonstration of "Christ in [us], the hope of glory" (Col. 1:27)? Yes, lost sinners who have been transformed by the power of God can propagate that hope to others. There will be a maturing of both good and evil so that every intelligent being can decide for themselves their eternal destiny.

The book of Revelation describes this very scenario. The maturing of the kingdom of the dragon and the manifestation of the principles and outworking of his government come to maturity in the image of the beast with the false prophet, and all of this is symbolized in the number 666 (see 13:18). This rebellious kingdom is in direct conflict with the maturing of the kingdom of Christ, the manifestation of His principles, and the outworking of His government, symbolized by the 144,000 (see 14:1).

The 144,000 are described as "having His Father's name written on their foreheads" (Rev. 14:1, NKJV). They are sons and daughters of God, possessing the character of Christ. They reflect the glory of the Father. "In their mouth was found no deceit, for they are without fault before the throne of God" (v. 5, NKJV). They are so filled with Christ, so enthralled with His beauty, that nothing this world has to offer can distract them from their purity of purpose. "They are virgins" (v. 4), sold out to Christ. Jesus is all in all to them. They accept no lord, bow to no authority, except Him who died for them, and His all-powerful Word. In the process of clinging to Jesus, beholding Jesus, loving Jesus, searching the Scriptures to hear Jesus' voice, and sharing Jesus with others, they have, unbeknown to themselves, come to reflect His character. They have "His name and the name of His Father written on their foreheads" (v. 1, NRSV).

With that said, what does one make of this strange phrase: they "follow the Lamb wherever he goes" (v. 4, NKJV). Where is Jesus going that they need to follow Him? We know that "we have such a High Priest, who is seated at the right hand of the throne of the Majesty in the heavens,

---

[3] Ellen G. White, Christ's Object Lessons (Washington, DC: Review and Herald Publishing Association, 1900), p. 69.

a Minister of the sanctuary and of the true tabernacle which the Lord erected and not man" (Heb. 8:1, 2, NKJV). According to our knowledge of Daniel 8:14, Jesus, our great high Priest, entered into the Most Holy Place in 1844, initiating the great antitypical day of atonement. There, in the Most Holy Place to this day, He mediates on behalf of the fallen sons and daughters of Adam for our salvation, "that your sins may be blotted out, when the times of refreshing shall come from the presence of the Lord" (Acts 3:19).

The Scripture is clear that soon—none know when, but soon indeed—Jesus is coming again as "KING OF KINGS AND LORD OF LORDS" (Rev. 19:16). He will appear riding on the cloud of glory with thousands upon thousands of His angels in triumphal procession (see Jude 14) to claim His bride and take her to the heavenly wedding feast. Sadly, painfully, the wicked will be destroyed at the brightness of His coming (see 2 Thess. 2:8). We see the harvest of the wheat and the destruction of the tares.

Yes, today Jesus is our Great High priest, ministering on our behalf before the throne of grace, soon to appear on the great white cloud as our King. Jesus, now our High Priest, will come as our King. But wait! If Jesus is our High Priest now and coming as our King, then before he can come as King, he must *become* King!

What an intriguing thought! Before he can come as King, he must become King. What does that look like in a practical sense? Jesus is a real person after all. Before Jesus can come as King, He must make the transition from His priestly ministration before the throne of grace to take His rightful place upon the throne of His kingdom. He must take off the vestments of His high priestly ministry and take up the crown of glory. He must lay aside the censer of mediation and take up the scepter of power.

Before Jesus can come as King, He must be enthroned as King. This change in Christ's ministration will become the epicenter of shockwaves that will roll through the universe. The transition from Priest to King—the exaltation of Jesus to the throne of the universe—will be the greatest paradigm shift this earth has seen since the fall of Adam. This event will rock the universe. A human being, the Son of man, exalted to the throne of God, will shake the heavens (see Hag. 2:6) and cause "a time of trouble, such as never was since there was a nation" (Dan. 12:1) here on earth.

The Scriptures state plainly, "[Jesus] must remain in heaven until the time of universal restoration" (Acts 3:21, NRSV). Could this event, the installation of the Son of man upon the throne of heaven as King, be the "restoration of all things" (NKJV)? Could the movement of Christ from his high-priestly position to kingship be the movement in heaven that explains why the 144,000 "follow the Lamb withersoever He goeth?" How could any kingdom come to completeness and maturity without the exaltation and revelation of its king? Didn't Jesus declare that "if I be lifted up from the earth, [I] will draw all men unto me" (John 12:32)?

Could the lifting up of Jesus to the throne in heaven be the "great day of the LORD" (Zeph. 1:14), the source and power of the final message of mercy that goes to all the earth before He comes? Is this the key that will unlock all the mysteries of last-day events? Could the coronation of the Son to reign with His Father upon the throne of the universe be the great event in heaven that initiates the closing scenes of this world's history?

This sounds exactly like what Jesus said: "Truly I tell you, at the renewal of all things, when the Son of Man is seated on the throne of his glory, you who have followed me will also sit on twelve thrones, judging the twelve tribes of Israel" (Matt. 19:28, NRSV). Peter stated that Jesus must remain in heaven until the restoration of all things. Jesus described the same thing—"the renewal of all things"—as the time or event "when the Son of Man is seated on the throne of his glory."

The great controversy in heaven began over the kingship of Christ. Lucifer, "the anointed cherub who covers" (Ezek. 28:14, NKJV), who stood in the presence of God, "little by little ... came to indulge the desire for self-exaltation." His "desire for supremacy" was accompanied by "envy of Christ."[4] The discontent grew until it became necessary for God to clearly set forth before the hosts of heaven the authority of His Son.

> The great Creator assembled the heavenly host, that He might in the presence of all the angels confer special honor upon His Son. The Son was seated on the throne with the Father ... The Father then made known that it was ordained by Himself that Christ, His Son, should be equal with Himself ... His Son He had invested with authority to command the heavenly host.[5]

---

[4] Ellen G. White, Patriarchs and Prophets (Washington, DC: Review and Herald Publishing Association, 1890), pp. 35, 37.
[5] Ellen G. White, The Story of Redemption (Washington, DC: Review and Herald Publishing Association, 1947), p. 13.

The installation of the Son of God upon the throne of the universe was the very event that caused the smoldering embers of envy and pride in Lucifer to burst into open flames of rebellion in heaven. "The exaltation of the Son of God as equal with the Father was represented as an injustice to Lucifer."[6]

The creation of this earth went forward to answer the objections and expose the false accusations of Satan. Mankind was created in the "image and likeness" of God, and to Adam was given "dominion" (Gen. 1:26, 28) over the earth. Humanity was to "have dominion over the fish of the sea, over the birds of the air, and over every living creature that moves on the earth" (v. 28, NKJV). The archdeceiver now bends his efforts toward erasing the visible evidence of God's glory in creation, thwarting His plan, and "to dispute the supremacy of the Son of God."[7] The prince of evil plans to usurp the kingship conferred upon Adam and thereby wrest the kingdom of this earth out of the hand of Christ. Satan gained the victory over Adam and claimed the world as his domain, exalting himself as the prince of this world, but his arrogant assertions were unfounded.

> *The installation of the Son of God upon the throne of the universe was the very event that caused the smoldering embers of envy and pride in Lucifer to burst into open flames of rebellion in heaven.*

> Satan's dominion was that wrested from Adam, but Adam was the vicegerent of the Creator. His was not an independent rule. The earth is God's, and He has committed all things to His Son. Adam was to reign subject to Christ. When Adam betrayed his sovereignty into Satan's hands, Christ still remained the rightful King.[8]

Satan's claim of dominion was a direct affront to his Creator in the battle with Christ over His kingship. The fall of Adam more directly brought the conflict over kingship down to this earth.

---

[6]Ellen G. White, Patriarchs and Prophets (Washington, DC: Review and Herald Publishing Association, 1890), p. 37.
[7]Ellen G. White, Patriarchs and Prophets (Washington, DC: Review and Herald Publishing Association, 1890), p. 38.
[8]Ellen G. White, The Desire of Ages (Mountain View, CA: Pacific Press Publishing Association, 1898), p. 129.

"Sorrow filled heaven, as it was realized that man was lost and that world which God had created was to be filled with mortals doomed to misery, sickness, and death, and there was no way of escape for the offender." Jesus would "take the sentence of death upon Himself, that through Him man might find pardon ... He would leave all his glory in heaven, and appear upon earth as a man."[9]

The Son of God would step down from the throne with His Father to expose the accusations of Satan against the kingdom of God and release the sons and daughters of Adam caught in the deceptions of the evil one. "Christ had come to disprove Satan's claim. ... The dominion that Adam had lost through sin would be recovered."[10]

"Satan again rejoiced with his angels that he could, by causing man's fall, pull down the Son of God from His exalted position. He told his angels that when Jesus should take fallen man's nature, he could overpower Him."[11]

Jesus "laid aside His crown and royal robe, and stepped down from the throne, to clothe His divinity with humanity."[12] He came down, down, down, plunging to the depths of our sin, degradation, and death. "Surely he has borne our griefs and carried our sorrows ... Smitten by God, and afflicted. But He was wounded for our transgressions, He was bruised for our iniquities. The chastisement for our peace was upon Him" (Isa. 53:4, 5, NKJV). "He made Him who knew no sin to be sin for us, that we might become the righteousness of God in him" (2 Cor. 5:21, NKJV). This is redemption's beautiful story.

From death's dark abyss, the Savior arose a conqueror at His resurrection. After appearing to the apostles, He ascended to heaven, giving the promise of His return in the same manner. Up, up, up, Jesus has ascended to where He now ministers as our Great High Priest in the Most Holy Place. The final step up to bring His ministration for the glory of His Father and the salvation of all that was lost full circle is His reinstatement back to the throne of the universe from whence He stepped down. Just as Jesus condescended and became like one of us, now He must be lifted up

---

[9]Ellen G. White, The Story of Redemption (Washington, DC: Review and Herald Publishing Association, 1947), pp. 42, 43.
[10]Ellen G. White, The Desire of Ages (Mountain View, CA: Pacific Press Publishing Association, 1898), p. 114.
[11]Ellen G. White, The Story of Redemption (Washington, DC: Review and Herald Publishing Association, 1947), p. 45.
[12]Ellen G. White, The Desire of Ages (Mountain View, CA: Pacific Press Publishing Association, 1898), p. 410.

to adorn His thorn-pierced brow with a golden crown and exchange the plain, white, linen garb of priesthood for the glorious, royal robes of kingship. He must take His rightful place as the great "I Am" upon the throne of the universe, clothing His humanity with His divinity, to be worshipped and adored by all creation.

"The restoration of all things" (Acts 3:21, NKJV) can only be accomplished with the restoration of the One who created all things. "In the beginning was the Word ... Through him all things were made; without him nothing was made that has been made" (John 1:1–3, NIV). Only when the Creator of all things takes His rightful place back upon the throne of the universe can "the restoration of all things" be realized. According to Acts 3:21, only after this event takes place will He return.

Could it be time? All the signs and events of our day tell us that "the kingdom of God is at hand" (Mark 1:15). Before Jesus can execute His authority and return as King, He must take His place on the throne of the universe and become King.

The King is be-coming! The KING is be-coming!!

Chapter 2

The King Becoming

In contemplating the glorious event of the second coming of our Lord Jesus Christ, the idea coalesced that before Jesus can come as King, He must *become* King. The "restitution of all things" (Acts 3:21, KJV) or "the regeneration," according to Jesus, is "when the Son of man shall sit in the throne of His glory" (Matt. 19:28). This restoration must occur before His advent takes place. Peter, speaking by inspiration of the Holy Spirit, said that Jesus "must remain in heaven until the time" (Acts 3:21, NRSV) this event takes place. Our conclusion that the restoration of all things in Acts 3:21 is the future installation of Christ as King is affirmed by the Spirit of Prophecy.

Mrs. White spoke of Christ's second coming: "The coming of Christ to usher in the reign of righteousness has inspired the most sublime and impassioned utterances of the sacred writers." She went on to quote a number of beautiful passages that speak of the glories of Christ's coming, then wrote, "About His coming cluster the glories of that 'restitution of all things, which God hath spoken by the mouth of all His holy prophets since the world began.' ... Then the long-continued rule of evil shall be broken; 'the kingdoms of this world' will become 'the kingdoms of our Lord, and of His Christ; and He shall reign for ever and ever.'"[13]

In this significant quote, she connected "the restitution of all things" with the seventh trumpet of Revelation 11:15, which describes Christ becoming King and beginning to reign. However, she was very particular with how she handled the text. Notice she didn't just quote the whole verse of Revelation 11:15; she changed the tense. The original verse states "are become" or "have become," a present tense form. Mrs. White changed this phrase to "will become," a future tense form. She connects "the restoration of all things" with the future event of the sounding of the seventh trumpet, when "He [Jesus] shall reign."

The conclusion that Jesus must become King before He comes as King is predicated on two absolute truths: Right now, Jesus is our Great High Priest ministering in the Most Holy Place for the salvation of His people (see Heb. 8:1, 2). Soon—very soon—He will come again. This is the blessed hope of His second coming. When He comes, He comes as "KING OF KINGS AND LORD OF LORDS" (Rev. 19:16). If Jesus, now our High Priest, is to come as the King of glory, then before He can come as King, He must *become* King.

> *We recognized that the onset of the great controversy between Lucifer and his Maker was over the kingship of Christ. It stands to reason then that the restoration of Jesus to the throne in heaven will be the final, climactic event that brings the conflict full circle, taking the war to a heightened frenzy here on earth before it closes.*

We recognized that the onset of the great controversy between Lucifer and his Maker was over the kingship of Christ. It stands to reason then that the restoration of Jesus to the throne in heaven will be the final, climactic event that brings the conflict full circle, taking the war to a heightened frenzy here on earth before it closes. Satan has been contending over the supremacy of Christ and His kingly authority for roughly six thousand years. The dragon will be enraged when "her child [is] caught up unto God, and to His throne" (Rev. 12:5), and the proclamation goes forth:

---
[13]Ellen G. White, The Great Controversy (Mountain View, CA: Pacific Press Publishing Association, 1911), pp. 300, 301.

"Now is come salvation, and strength, and the kingdom of our God, and the power of His Christ" (v. 10). Satan can't interrupt the events in heaven, but he can attack Christ's subjects on earth. "The dragon was wroth with the woman and went to make war with the remnant of her seed, which keep the commandments of God and have the testimony of Jesus Christ" (v. 17). Thus, the stage is set for the final scenes of the conflict of the ages.

The thesis of the installation of Christ as King raises many questions that beg for answers. However, before we jump to conclusions and start discussing the ramifications of such a paradigm shift, we need to verify that this is what the Bible teaches and is not just human imaginings.

Is it truth or just human logic? Does the plain teaching of the Scriptures supply evidence to affirm the thesis? Yes, the Bible teaches that Jesus is our High Priest in heaven (see Heb. 8:1–5). Yes, the Bible teaches that Jesus is coming again (see John 14:1–3). Yes, it teaches that when He comes, He will be "KING OF KINGS AND LORD OF LORDS" (Rev. 19:16). With that said, does the Bible anywhere describe the process of Jesus becoming King that will give us insight as to how, when, and what it means to us who are waiting for His return? More specifically, does the Bible prophesy about the transition in ministration where the acting High Priest actually becomes installed as the King? Let us consider the word of the Lord through the prophet:

> Then the word of the LORD came to me, saying: "Receive *the gift* from the captives—from Heldai, Tobijah, and Jedaiah, who have come from Babylon—and go the same day and enter the house of Josiah the son of Zephaniah. Take the silver and gold, make an elaborate crown, and set *it* on the head of Joshua the son of Jehozadak, the high priest. Then speak to him, saying, 'Thus says the LORD of hosts, saying: "Behold, the Man whose name *is* the BRANCH! From His place He shall branch out, And He shall build the temple of the LORD; Yes, He shall build the temple of the LORD. He shall bear the glory, And shall sit and rule on His throne; So He shall be a priest on His throne, And the counsel of peace shall be between them both."' "Now the elaborate crown shall be for a memorial in the temple of the LORD for Helem, Tobijah, Jedaiah, and Hen the son of Zephaniah. Even those from afar shall come and build the temple of the LORD. Then you shall know that the LORD of hosts has sent Me to you. And *this* shall come to pass if you

diligently obey the voice of the Lord your God." (Zechariah 6:9–15, NJKV).

In this prophetic vision given to Zechariah, Joshua, the acting high priest, is crowned as king and takes His place on the throne to rule (see v. 13). This event causes a worldwide gathering; people from "afar shall come and build the temple of the LORD" (v. 15). Just one short comment before we revisit the passage: "Joshua" is Hebrew for the Greek name "Jesus." With that in mind, let's read the passage again, but with your permission, I will add the name that is above all names to exalt Him to His rightful place.

> Then the word of the LORD came to me saying: "Receive the gift from the captives—from Heldai, Tobijah, and Jedaiah, who have come from Babylon—and go the same day and enter the house of Josiah the son of Zephaniah. Take the silver and gold, make an elaborate crown, and set it on the head of [Jesus] the son of Jehozadak,[14] the high priest. Then speak to him, saying, 'Thus says the LORD of hosts, saying: "Behold, the Man [Jesus] whose name is the BRANCH! From His place [Jesus] shall branch out, And [Jesus] shall build the temple of the LORD; Yes, [Jesus] shall build the temple of the LORD. [Jesus] shall bear the glory, And [Jesus] shall sit and rule on His throne; [Jesus] shall be a priest on His throne, And the counsel of peace shall be between them both."' "Now the elaborate crown shall be for a memorial in the temple of the LORD for Helem, Tobijah, Jedaiah, and Hen the son of Zephaniah. Even those from afar shall come and build the temple of the LORD. Then you shall know that the Lord of hosts has sent Me to you. And this shall come to pass if you diligently obey the voice of the Lord your God."

Does this answer our question about the Bible prophesying the event of the High Priest becoming King? Could the Scriptures be any more specific about the transition in ministration where the acting High Priest becomes installed as the King? Could the prophecy be any more direct identifying that Jesus is the acting High Priest who is to be crowned and seated on the throne as King? Therefore, it is more than just common-sense logic that before Jesus can come as King, he must become King. It is a scripturally based theology revealing the final phase of the heavenly ministration of

---

[14] "Jehozadak" comes from *Jehovah sedeq*, which means "God of righteousness."

Christ in the fulfillment of the plan of salvation. This remarkable prophecy is intriguing, inviting us to investigate further.

Zechariah is straightforward and to the point, but according to the Scriptures, everything must be established by the testimony of at least two witnesses (see Matt. 18:16). Is there scriptural support for Zechariah's prophecy of the kingship of Jesus in the symbolism of the Branch in 6:12? Who is the Branch? Let the Scripture interpret itself:

> "Behold, *the* days are coming," says the LORD, "That I will raise to David a Branch of righteousness; A King shall reign and prosper, And execute judgment and righteousness in the earth. In His days Judah will be saved, And Israel will dwell safely; Now this *is* His name by which He will be called: THE LORD OUR RIGHTEOUSNESS." (Jeremiah 23:5, 6, NKJV)

Jeremiah and Zechariah's testimonies of the Branch corroborate with each other. The "raising" of the Branch is the installation of One who is a son of David to the throne. One who is not yet king becomes King; "A King shall reign." He will "execute judgment and righteousness." "In his days Judah will be saved." Is there any question that Jesus is "THE LORD OUR RIGHTEOUSNESS" to whom Jeremiah refers? Jeremiah affirms that Jesus is the Branch, the Son of David, who is to become the King that shall reign. Isaiah joins the chorus and testifies of the Branch.

> There shall come forth a Rod from the stem of Jesse, And a Branch shall grow out of his roots. The Spirit of the LORD shall rest upon Him, The Spirit of wisdom and understanding, The Spirit of counsel and might, The Spirit of knowledge and of the fear of the LORD. His delight *is* in the fear of the LORD, And He shall not judge by the sight of His eyes, Nor decide by the hearing of His ears; But with righteousness He shall judge the poor, And decide with equity for the meek of the earth; He shall strike the earth with the rod of His mouth, And with the breath of His lips He shall slay the wicked. Righteousness shall be the belt of His loins, And faithfulness the belt of His waist. (Isaiah 11:1–5, NKJV)

The harmony of these references concerning the Branch, who He is, what His role or function is, and what that means is clear, convincing, and decisive. Jesus is to become King. Jeremiah's, Isaiah's, and Zechariah's testimonies corroborate regarding a Christ event that marks a huge paradigm shift in the ministration in heaven. We have not yet discussed the details in these prophecies that begin to explain the ramifications of such a momentous event. We are simply verifying the plausibility from the Scriptures that Christ's kingship is a heavenly event that is prophesied to happen. This movement in heaven—the Branch becoming King (see Zech. 6), THE LORD OUR RIGHTEOUSNESS beginning to reign (see Jer. 23; Isa. 11) —corresponds with a movement on the earth. Each of the three scriptural references identifies the movement of Him becoming King and connects it to a movement on earth: a gathering of the peoples of the world, a calling of people out of Babylon. Zechariah stated:

> Receive the gift from the captives—from Heldai, Tobijah, and Jedaiah, who have come from Babylon ... Now the elaborate crown shall be for a memorial in the temple of the LORD for Helem, Tobijah, Jedaiah, and Hen the son of Zephaniah. Even those from afar shall come and build the temple of the LORD. (Zechariah 6:10, 14, 15, NKJV).

Jeremiah described it this way:

> "Therefore behold, the days are coming," says the LORD, "that they shall no longer say, 'As the LORD lives who brought up the children of Israel from the land of Egypt,' but, 'As the LORD lives who brought up and led the descendants of the house of Israel from the north country and from all the countries where I had driven them.' And they shall dwell in their own land." (Jeremiah 23:7, 8, NKJV).

And Isaiah declared:

> "And in that day there shall be a Root of Jesse, Who shall stand as a banner to the people; For the Gentiles shall seek Him, And His resting place shall be glorious." It shall come to pass in that day *That* the Lord shall set His hand again the second time To recover the remnant of His people who are left, From Assyria and Egypt, From Pathros and Cush, From Elam and Shinar, From Hamath and the islands of the sea. He will set up a banner for the nations, And will assemble the outcasts of Israel, And gather together the dispersed of Judah From the four corners of the earth. (Isaiah 11:10–12, NKJV)

Not only does Scripture prophesy that Jesus our High Priest will become King, but that this movement in heaven will initiate a movement on earth, a calling and gathering of people out of Babylon that will complete the process of the Messiah's ministration to build the house of the Lord. The Branch completes the work of salvation. The restoration of Him to the throne, His rightful and original place of authority, is the restoration of all things. The completion is found in Him. He is "THE LORD OUR RIGHTEOUSNESS" (Jer. 23:6).

A question arises as to the fulfilment of the prophecy of Zechariah. Wasn't Jesus inaugurated as Priest and King at Pentecost, when he became a High Priest according to the order of Melchizedek (see Heb. 5:5)? Then wouldn't the Pentecost event of AD 31 be the fulfilment of the prophecy of "a priest upon the throne" that brings peace between them both? Let's look a little closer at the context in Zechariah to see if it can give us any insight to discern the timing of the event of the High Priest being made King.

Zechariah saw Joshua, the High Priest, "standing before the angel of the LORD, and Satan standing at his right hand to resist him … Now Joshua was clothed in filthy garments, and stood before the angel" (3:1, 3). The vision moves forward, the filthy garments are removed, and Joshua is clothed with "rich robes" (v. 4, NKJV).

There are four places in Scripture where the priests are directed to change their garments (see Lev. 6:10, 11; 16:4, 23, 24, 32; Ezek. 42:14; 44:19). The first reference concerns "the law of the burnt offering" (Lev. 6:9). Here the priest is directed to change his garments while removing the ashes from the alter. This reference has no connection with our prophecy besides the changing of the garment. Ezekiel 42:14 and 44:19 deal with the priest taking off his holy vestments and leaving them within the sacred precincts of the temple.

This is the opposite of Zechariah. In Zechariah, the initial vestments are filthy, and clean or holy vestments are put on the priest. The only other place in Scripture where the high priest changes his garments is found in Leviticus 16:23–24. Here, Aaron is instructed to "take off the linen garments," "wash his body with water," and "put on his garments" (NKJV). This reference fits the context in Zechariah because 1) it's specific to the high priest, not just to priests in general, and 2) it describes a cleansing process, from filthy to clean. Leviticus 16 is a detailed description of the Day of Atonement liturgy.

Zechariah also saw Joshua the high priest standing before God, bearing the sin of all the people, and "saith the Lord of hosts, and I will remove the iniquity of that land in one day" (3:9). The removing of the iniquity in a single day is another reference to the Day of Atonement. "For on that day shall the priest make an atonement for you, to cleanse you, that ye may be clean from all your sins before the LORD" (Lev. 16:30).

The clean garments in the place of filthy ones and the cleansing of the iniquity of the land in a single day is Day of Atonement language. This was the most solemn day of the Jewish calendar, when the sins of Israel were purged and the temple and camp were cleansed of all iniquity. According to the scriptural context, Zechariah was describing the high priest in the process of cleansing the temple on the Day of Atonement in the Most Holy Place, when he is taken, crowned king, and set upon the throne to rule (6:12, 13).

Mrs. White affirmed this truth in her commentary on these verses. "'He showed me Joshua the high priest standing before the Angel of the Lord, and Satan standing at his right hand to resist him.' Jesus is our great High Priest in heaven. And what is he doing? He is making intercession and atonement for his people who believe in Him."[15]

After explaining the corporate application of Zechariah's vision of Joshua and the Angel to ancient Israel and the personal application to us, Mrs. White quoted, "'Take away the filthy garments, and clothe him with change of raiment, and set a fair miter upon his head.' ... Zechariah's vision of Joshua and the Angel applies with peculiar force to the experience of God's people in the closing up of the great day of atonement. The remnant church will be brought into great trial and distress."[16] More than merely applying the prophecy to the end-time day of atonement, she specifically applied it to the *closing* of it.

The scriptural context of Zechariah and the testimony of the Spirit of Prophecy affirm that Zechariah's prophecy of our High Priest becoming King occurs in the context of His day of atonement ministration. We know that Christ's high-priestly, day of atonement ministration in the Most Holy Place began in 1844. Therefore, the prophecy of Zechariah cannot have been fulfilled at Pentecost in AD 31. The Pentecostal inauguration of AD 31 anointed Christ as priest so he could begin His priestly ministration in

---

[15]Ellen G. White, Testimonies to Ministers and Gospel Workers (Mountain View, CA: Pacific Press Publishing Association, 1923), p. 37.

[16]Ellen G. White, Testimonies for the Church, vol. 5 (Mountain View, CA: Pacific Press Publishing Association, 1889), p. 472.

the Holy Place, walking among the seven golden lampstands, as revealed to John circa AD 90 (see Rev. 1). Zechariah describes an event that takes place during the antitypical day of atonement, exalting an already existing and ministering High Priest to the throne as King. This prophecy can only be fulfilled sometime after 1844.

Since 1844, Jesus our Great High Priest is ministering in the Most Holy Place on this antitypical day of atonement. According to the prophecy of Zechariah, at some point during His high priestly ministration before the throne, the Father will call Him to sit down on the throne and crown him as King. Our High Priest will become the newly installed King, then Jesus can and will come as "KING OF KINGS AND LORD OF LORDS" (Rev. 19:16).

> *According to the prophesies, this great movement in heaven will be accompanied by a great final movement on the earth, more powerful than Pentecost, more moving than the Millerites, to prepare a people for the coming of the King.*

According to the previous quote, Mrs. White described this event as "the closing up of the great day of atonement," which will bring "great trial and distress" on God's remnant church. According to the prophesies, this great movement in heaven will be accompanied by a great final movement on the earth, more powerful than Pentecost, more moving than the Millerites, to prepare a people for the coming of the King.

The prophecy of the Branch in Zechariah is describing exactly the scenario about which we are talking. "Hear O Joshua, the high priest, You and your companions who sit before you, For they are a wondrous sign; For behold, I am bringing forth My Servant the BRANCH" (Zech. 3:8, NKJV).

The Spirit of Prophecy affirms the fact that the coronation of Christ as King is a future, day of atonement, after-1844 event, not a historic, AD-31, Pentecost event.

> We are called now to be educated, that we may do the work that God has assigned to us, and it will not crush out our life. The humblest can have a share in the work, and a share in the reward when the coronation shall take place, and Christ, our Advocate

and Redeemer, becomes the King of His redeemed subjects. We must now do all in our power to seek personal consecration to God. It is not more mighty men, not more talented men, not more learned men, that we need in the presentation of the truth for this time; but men who have a knowledge of God and Jesus Christ, whom He has sent.[17]

The plain teaching of the Scriptures supplies evidence to affirm our thesis that Jesus, our High Priest in the heavens, will become King before He comes as King. Zechariah saw in vision the transition in ministration where the acting High Priest, in the midst of His day of atonement ministration, is installed as the King. In the biblical symbolism of the Branch from multiple prophetic witnesses, we have seen the plain teaching of Scripture. This evidence, supported by clear statements from the Spirit of Prophecy and by common sense, affirms our thesis.

Jesus, our great High Priest, is now ministering on this antitypical day of atonement in the Most Holy Place. Soon, the Father will call Him to sit down on the throne, place upon Him the crown, and confer upon Him the kingship. "He shall bear the glory, And shall sit and rule on His throne; So He shall be a priest on His throne, And the counsel of peace shall be between them both" (Zech. 6:13, NKJV). Yes, before Jesus comes as King, He must become King.

The King is be-coming! The KING is be-coming!!

---

[17]Ellen G. White, Ye Shall Receive Power (Hagerstown, MD: Review and Herald Publishing Association, 1995), p. 182

Chapter 3

Prophesy Again

The second coming of Christ is a revelation of the King. Every child in Sabbath School knows Jesus comes as King. The idea that before Jesus can come as King, He must *become* King, seems like common sense. However, just thinking through the transition, one comes to realize that this will be a huge paradigm shift that will impact every being in heaven and the earth. In 1844, Jesus moved from the Holy to the Most Holy in heaven, igniting a movement that became a firestorm of religious fervor not seen since the Reformation.

Imagine what it will mean when Jesus, having been exalted to the throne of the universe, adored by all creation as the King of glory, begins the process of coming out of the heavenly sanctuary to return to earth to receive His people. Thousands of angels will sing, "Worthy is the Lamb who was slain To receive power and riches and wisdom, And strength and honor and glory and blessing!" (Rev. 5:12, NKJV). What will be the response of the dragon and the kings of this earth? Will they be so eager to relinquish their right to rule to the newly installed King? This Christ event will have catastrophic ramifications. Everything that can be shaken will be shaken. Could the convulsions we see in nature and society be evidence that the event is even at the door?

The reality of the second coming, that Christ comes as King, is historic Adventist doctrine and common biblical knowledge. Zechariah established a scriptural authority for the specific prophetic event of the transition in ministration. He saw Joshua the high priest, representing Jesus, during his Day of Atonement ministry, being crowned and placed on the throne as king. Jeremiah and Isaiah affirmed the "Branch" symbolism as kingship imagery. All three prophets identify a movement on earth that corresponds to this movement in heaven. There is a myriad of questions, similar to the one we addressed about Pentecost, that this thesis raises, but before we start talking about the ramifications of such an event, there is a need to firmly establish a sound Biblical foundation for this Christ event. To do so, we have to determine the line of reasoning by which to further research this subject. How should we proceed?

We are talking about the reality of Christ's second coming. The idea that Jesus becomes King before He can come as King is new to some, but really, we are defining the steps in the process of what we call the second coming. Therefore, why not follow the lead of the experts who went before us? Why not go back to our foundations? The founders of the Advent movement spent a lot of time and energy studying the second coming of Jesus in the Scriptures to prepare a people for the event. We know that God was leading them.

Speaking of William Miller, Mrs. Whites wrote, "God sent His angel ... to lead him to search the prophecies ... to guide his mind and open to his understanding prophecies which had ever been dark to God's people. The commencement of the chain of truth was given to him." Miller faithfully studied the prophecies and saw that he was "living in the closing scenes of this world's history."[18]

We are Seventh-day Adventists. The Seventh-day Adventist movement grew out of the Millerite Advent movement and the Great Disappointment of 1844. To this day, we uphold the validity of Miller's understandings of the prophecies and the accuracy of his message. The Millerite movement was spot-on in every aspect except the misunderstanding of the event that would happen at the close of the 2,300 days.

> The advent movement of 1840-44 was a glorious manifestation of the power of God; the first angel's message was carried to every missionary station in the world, and in some countries there was

---

[18]Ellen G. White, Early Writings (Washington, DC: Review and Herald Publishing Association, 1882), p. 229.

the greatest religious interest which had been witnessed in any land since the Reformation of the sixteenth century; but these are to be exceeded by the mighty movement under the last warning of the third angel.[19]

The Advent movement was a glorious manifestation of the power of God, generating the greatest religious interest since the Reformation. Why should we shy away from our roots when we know that the events were inspired by God? Why not stand on the shoulders of the spiritual giants who have gone before us to see if we can catch a view of what's over the horizon?

Revelation 10 is a foundational truth to us as Seventh-day Adventists. Miller's message and movement, as ordained by God, was sweet in the mouth but bitter in the stomach (see v. 10). The Great Disappointment was prophesied ahead of time to encourage and affirm the disappointed saints to not turn back, but to go forward. The prophecy ends with a command from the angel: "Thou must prophesy again" (v. 11). Since we are the "descendants" of the Millerite movement, the command to prophesy again must be directed to us. We must prophesy again!

What does it mean to "prophesy again?" We have traditionally accepted it to mean that the Seventh-day Adventist Church is to proclaim the three angels' messages to the world to prepare a people for the second coming of Jesus. That's true, but what if the command is more specific than that? What if it means that the whole Millerite experience needs to happen again? What Miller studied to come to his understandings needs to be studied again. The three angels' messages need to be sounded again. The convicting power of God needs to accompany the message again. The message needs to become a movement again.

Can "prophesy again" mean to do the same thing they did ... again? The "again" concept is repeated by Mrs. White regarding this topic.

---
[19]Ellen G. White, The Great Controversy (Mountain View, CA: Pacific Press Publishing Association, 1911), p. 611.

"The power which stirred the people so mightily in the 1844 movement will again be revealed."[20] The call to prophesy again, as commanded by the angel of Revelation 10, is the line of reasoning that we will follow to research the subject of Jesus becoming King.

Based on the command to prophesy again, we will follow in the path of William Miller and look for the Lord's leading. If Jesus becoming King is the next great event that is to occur, then surely the same prophecies that guided Miller's understanding will also provide insight for us on whom the end of the ages has come.

Miller methodically demonstrated the flow of earthly history from the kingdom of Babylon down to his day through the image of Nebuchadnezzar's dream in Daniel 2, confirming it from Daniel's vision of the beasts in chapter 7. He was able to demonstrate simply and clearly where they were in the stream of prophetic time. The prophecies of Daniel 2 and 7 laid the foundation for Miller's understanding of prophetic time. This is where he started; this is where we will start.

There were two prophetic scenes, more than any other, that became the engine that drove the Millerite movement and have become the heritage of the Seventh-day Adventist message: the three angels' messages of Revelation 14 were the engine that powered the movement; the bittersweet prophecy of Revelation 10 that explained the great disappointment preserved the validity of the message. Both played a pivotal role in the Millerite message and became the calling and purpose of the Seventh-day Adventist movement. Heeding the heavenly command to prophesy again, we will revisit these prophecies to see if they can shed any light on our thesis.

The command to prophesy again is more than facts and figures. Miller's burden and the power of his message was the sober call to each person to make oneself ready to meet Jesus. The convicting power of the Holy Spirit attended his message; revival and reform followed in its train. Ellen White, commenting on the experience, wrote, "Everywhere were souls in deep anguish pleading with God. Many wrestled all night in prayer for the assurance that their own sins were pardoned, or for the conversion of their relatives or neighbors."[21] Moreover:

> The sincere believers carefully examined every thought and emotion of their hearts as if upon their deathbeds and in a few hours

---
[20]Ellen G. White, Testimonies for the Church, vol. 5 (Mountain View, CA: Pacific Press Publishing Association, 1889), p. 252.
[21]Ellen G. White, The Great Controversy (Mountain View, CA: Pacific Press Publishing Association, 1911), p. 369.

to close their eyes upon earthly scenes. There was no making of "ascension robes" ... but all felt the need of internal evidence that they were prepared to meet the Saviour; their white robes were purity of soul--characters cleansed from sin by the atoning blood of Christ. Would that there were still with the professed people of God the same spirit of heart searching, the same earnest, determined faith.[22]

Another who participated in the movement testified: "It produced everywhere the most deep searching of heart and humiliation of soul before the God of high heaven. It caused a weaning of affections from the things of this world, a healing of controversies and animosities, a confession of wrongs, a breaking down before God, and penitent, brokenhearted supplications to Him for pardon and acceptance. It caused self-abasement and prostration of soul, such as we never before witnessed."[23]

Summarizing the experience, Mrs. White stated, "The fruits of the advent movement, the spirit of humility and heart searching, of renouncing of the world and reformation of life, which attended the work, testified that it was of God."[24] This same spirit of intense, earnest, honest heart-searching must accompany our search of the Scriptures if we are to prophesy again. How can we study the process of Christ's coming and not engage in the process of preparing for His coming? We need the same Spirit of conviction and power that accompanied Miller as he proclaimed the hour of God's judgment. The three angels' messages were the basis of the Millerite message (see *The Great Controversy*, p. 611, quoted above).

The Seventh-day Adventist Church was once a movement proclaiming present truth. It was a movement on earth because it was following the movement of Christ in heaven. It was proclaiming present truth because it was a present-truth message about Jesus, who He is, where He is, what He is doing, and its impact on the great controversy that is being played out on this dark planet. Is it not time to prophesy again? Is it not time for the Seventh-day Adventist Church to become a movement again?

This line of reasoning that has been chosen for our study of the kingship of Christ is in harmony with the counsel of the Spirit of Prophecy: "Study Revelation in connection with Daniel; for history will be repeated.... We,

---

[22]Ibid., p. 373.
[23]Ibid., p. 401.
[24]Ibid., p. 405.

with all our religious advantages, ought to know far more today than we do know."²⁵ "If the books of Daniel and the Revelation were studied with earnest prayer, we should have a better knowledge of the perils of the last days, and would be better prepared for the work before us-we should be prepared to unite with Christ and to work in his lines."²⁶

These statements, penned by Mrs. White in 1904, are surprising and challenging. What does she mean "we ought to know far more today," and should we be prepared to unite with Christ and work in His lines? Could it be that the very prophecies that sparked the Advent movement to life in the past contain insights to awaken a sleepy Laodicean church to a dynamic movement again? In the words of the Spirit of Prophecy:

> When we as a people understand what this book [Daniel] means to us, there will be seen among us a great revival. We do not understand fully the lessons that it teaches, notwithstanding the injunction given us to search and study it.²⁷
>
> Those who eat the flesh and drink the blood of the Son of God will bring from the books of Daniel and Revelation truth that is inspired by the Holy Spirit. They will start into action forces that cannot be repressed.²⁸

If Christ's movement in heaven from the Holy Place into the Most Holy Place in 1844 was accompanied by the greatest religious revival on earth since the Reformation, then how much more will the transition of Christ becoming King in heaven and his movements out of the heavenly sanctuary back to earth be accompanied by a much greater reformation and revival movement? We have been told that "the power which stirred the people so mightily in the 1844 movement will again be revealed."²⁹

Following the command to prophesy again, we will study the prophecies Daniel 2, 7, Revelation 10, 14 to see if the next Christ event that is to occur is the King be-coming.

---

[25] Ellen G. White, Testimonies to Ministers and Gospel Workers (Mountain View, CA: Pacific Press Publishing Association, 1923), p. 116.
[26] Ellen G. White, "The Prayer That God Accepts," The Review and Herald, February 9, 1897.
[27] Ellen G. White, Testimonies to Ministers and Gospel Workers (Mountain View, CA: Pacific Press Publishing Association, 1923), p. 113.
[28] Ibid., p. 116.
[29] Ellen G. White, Testimonies for the Church, vol. 5 (Mountain View, CA: Pacific Press Publishing Association, 1889), p. 252.

Chapter 4
The Son of Man

The Lord opened William Miller's mind to understand the prophecies. "The commencement of the chain of truth was given to him, and he was led on to search for link after link, until he looked with wonder and admiration upon the Word of God. He saw there a perfect chain of truth."[30] Encouraged by the counsel to study Revelation in connection with Daniel and dwell much on the prophecies and scenes brought to view in these books, we will study Daniel 7 to see if there is a link in the chain of truth that shines light on our time.

Daniel 7 is the cornerstone of the historical interpretation of apocalyptic prophecy. Its chronological sequence of kingdoms, understood in conjunction with the image of Nebuchadnezzar's dream in chapter 2, identifies the sequence of world kingdoms from Babylon down to our time. These two visions, more than any other, laid the groundwork for Miller's understanding of our place in the stream of prophetic time. The vision of Daniel 7 is the anchor for the Adventist historicist understanding of end-time prophecies. This is why we are counseled to study it.

---

[30]Ellen G. White, Early Writings (Washington, DC: Review and Herald Publishing Association, 1882), p. 229.

How will we know unless, like Miller, we diligently study the Scriptures for ourselves?[31] Let's prayerfully go to Daniel 7 and listen to the Word of God. "Daniel spoke, saying, 'I saw in my vision by night, and behold, the four winds of heaven were stirring up the Great sea. And four great beasts came up out of the sea, each different from the other'" (vs. 2, 3, NKJV).

Daniel's introduction of the vision lays the conceptual foundation for the whole chapter. The word picture that is painted becomes the theatrical setting in which the vision unfolds. This backdrop creates the environment for the introduction of each of the players, in each scene, and supplies the overall understanding of the relational dynamics between the scenes.

Daniel is in vision at night and sees the four winds of heaven stirring up the great sea. The introduction contains three key components that give us the literary clues to determine the overall context of the vision. The three basic components are night, winds, and sea. These symbols individually could be taken to mean most anything, but together they present a biblical pattern that directs our attention to the conceptual foundation of the vision. The pattern of the three elements is a direct reference to creation history in Genesis 1: "And the earth was without form, and void; and darkness was upon the face of the deep. And the Spirit of God moved upon the face of the waters" (v. 2).

It is common, Eastern, cyclical thought that you end where you started. Since the Bible is an Eastern book, it's not surprising that it describes the end by referring us to the beginning.

Daniel 7:2	Genesis 1:2
Night	Darkness
Winds	Spirit
Sea	Waters

The combination of these elements in the introduction of the vision presents creation as the overall concept for the revelation. God refers us to the beginning to describe the end. It is common, Eastern, cyclical thought that you end where you started. Since the Bible is an Eastern book, it's not surprising that it describes the end by referring us to the beginning. Cyclical thought is not just an out-of-place, ancient Eastern

---
[31]See Ellen G. White, Gospel Workers (Washington, DC: Review and Herald Publishing Association, 1915), p. 299.

concept. Jesus presents Himself to His church as the "Alpha and Omega, the beginning and the end" (Rev. 21:6). Foreshadowing the end by the beginning and describing the beginning to define the end constitute sound, Christ-centered theology. He is "the first and the last" (22:13). Seeing creation in Genesis 1 as the context and conceptual foundation of Daniel's vision of the end is not only sound, biblical prophetic interpretation, in harmony with the ancient thought patterns well known to our author, but sound Christological interpretation.

The symbol of "the four winds" (Dan. 7:2) is consistently employed by God in Scripture to convey a message to a prophet in vision (see Zech. 2:6, 6:5; Dan. 7:2, 8:8, 11:4; Rev. 7:2). Ezekiel 37 is the clearest reference to interpret the meaning of the symbol of the four winds. Ezekiel is brought to the valley of dry bones and asked if these bones could live. He's then commanded to prophesy to the bones. "Thus saith the Lord GOD; Come from the four winds, O breath, and breathe upon these slain, that they may live" (v. 9). The Spirit that brings life to the dry bones is described to Ezekiel as coming from "the four winds."

Only the Creator can take that which is dead and give it life. This is creation symbolism. The four winds are employed as a symbol in vision to the prophet to convey the idea of the Creator being active in creation. The action of creation may be viewed as positive or negative from the creatures' perspectives, depending on their relationships to the Creator. Therefore, the symbol of the four winds in Scripture is presented as both positive and negative in various places. A new creation for believers is positive and desirable; for the wicked it is disruptive and destructive. This insight might be helpful for those wrestling to understand the context of the other references given, but the point being made here is that the symbol of the four winds is a reference to creation.

The biblical pattern of night, winds, and water drawn from Genesis 1 and the symbolism of the four winds combine in the introduction of Daniel 7 to present creation as the context of the vision. Creation is not occurring in a vacuum. There is a conflict dynamic accentuated in Daniel's vision that reflects the drama in Genesis 1. In Genesis, the darkness and chaotic waters are presented as obstacles the Creator must overcome to cause order where it is formless and void.

Daniel 7 picks up on this dynamic of conflict in the context of creation. The four winds of heaven are "stirring up the Great sea" (v. 2, NKJV). This phrase conveys the idea of laboring to bring forth. The Septuagint is more emphatic on this point. It translates the verse, "the four winds of heaven blew violently upon the great sea."[32] The Spirit of God, represented by the four winds of heaven, is laboring to bring forth order, but the great sea is resisting creation. How does the sea resist?

"And four great beasts came up from the sea" (v. 3). The origin of the beasts from the sea is evidence of their harmony of spirit and purpose. That they come up out of the chaotic water conveys the idea of being exalted to positions of authority, even set forth as defenders of the realm. This concept to "come up" relating to exaltation and authority is imbedded in the imagery that surrounds each of the beasts in their description. The Lion is "lifted up" (v. 4), the bear is "raised up" (v. 5), and the leopard is given "dominion" (v. 6). The same phrase is used to describe the positioning of the little horn: it "came up" (v. 8) when it exalts itself as God. A horn itself is a symbol of kingship (see Rev. 17:12). The four beasts are exalting themselves to positions of authority, becoming kings of their domain. This is not speculation. Later, Daniel requests an explanation from an angel and is told, "These great beasts, which are four, are four kings, which shall arise out of the earth" (7:17). It sounds like we are on the right trail of our topic.

These four beast-kings become the personification of the sea's resistance to the Creator's will. The four beasts are the antitheses of the four winds. The conflict is demonstrated in the structure of the verse. Heaven is in direct conflict with the sea. The Spirit of God is striving with the chaotic waters, which are peoples, multitudes, nations, and languages (see Rev. 17:15). The four winds that personify heaven are set in antithetical contrast to the four beasts that personify the sea. This conflict is demonstrated in the struggle between the winds and the beasts. The Spirit strives with the flesh; the flesh strives with the Spirit. The conflict in Daniel 7:2–3 is structured like this:

    A—the four winds
        B—of heaven
            C—stirring up
                X—the Great Sea and
    A—four great beasts
        B—from the sea
            C—came up

---

[32]Sir Lancelot C.L. Brenton, The Septuagint with Apocrypha: Greek and English (Peabody, MA: Hendrickson Publishers, 1992), p. 1060.

The evidence of the harmony in the purpose of the four beasts with the sea is composed of more than just their origin. The beasts share the title "great" with the sea from which they arose. The titles "great sea" and "great beasts" reveal the principle motive behind their actions. The understanding of the term "great" is clarified in the context by its parallel application to the little horn, which has a mouth that speaks "great things [or words]" (vs. 8, 11, 20, 25). In Daniel 2, the "great image" is in conflict with the "great mountain" (vs. 31, 35). In chapter 4, Nebuchadnezzar boasts about the "great Babylon" that he had built (see v. 30).

> *These kings are described as beasts because they function by the lusts of the flesh. Their kingdoms are founded on selfish, oppressive principles of fear and coercive control. They are predacious beasts because they exploit the lifeblood of any of those who are weaker, subject to their control, or viewed as a threat in an attempt to exalt themselves and maintain their authority.*

In each case, the term "great," attributed to a creature, describes the attitude of one exalting itself above God, laying claim to prerogatives that belong to the Creator alone. The creature is in conflict with its Maker. This is the controversy over who is "great," more familiar to us as "the great controversy." The term "great," attached to the names of the sea and the beasts that come up from it, is a definitive statement of the rebellious nature of the creatures exalting themselves against their Creator, resisting His will and rejecting His creative authority to bring all things in harmony with Himself.

The overall concept of the vision depicted through the word picture etched by Daniel is the process of the Creator bringing order to the realm of chaos. God initiates creation, or recreation, in the context of the great controversy drama. Creatures, resisting the Creator's will and rejecting His authority, exalt themselves against their Maker. "He opposes and exalts himself above every so-called god or object of worship, so that he takes his seat in the temple of God, declaring himself to be God" (2 Thess. 2:4, NRSV).

These kings are described as beasts because they function by the lusts of the flesh. Their kingdoms are founded on selfish, oppressive principles of fear and coercive control. They are predacious beasts because they exploit the lifeblood of any of those who are weaker, subject to their control, or viewed as a threat in an attempt to exalt themselves and maintain their authority. The fang, claw, and horn become the enforcement of the beast principle to coerce others to conform to their standards. Thus, the lion, bear, leopard, and "dragon" are fit symbols of ferocious beasts that feed upon the suppression of others and raise themselves up by standing upon the corpses of those they have exploited. The four beasts strive to maintain their dominion through the fear of death (see Heb. 2:15) in a fallen, chaotic world of survival of the fittest.

The number "4" describes the extent of the conflict. The four winds go forth to cause order in the four corners of the earth. The four great beasts, the antitheses of the four winds, come up out of the great sea, resisting the Creator and creation at every point. "Four" denotes the cardinal points of the compass, meaning that the conflict encompasses the whole earth, in terms of both time and space. The beasts of Daniel 7 follow the same pattern of the metals of the image of chapter 2, describing the kingdoms of this world from Daniel's time down to the end. This historical position has great strength of merit in light of all the supportive evidence available. The symbols in Daniel 7 have been correctly identified by the historical record as:

- Lion—Babylon (605 BC–539 BC)
- Bear—Medo-Persia (539 BC–331 BC)
- Leopard—Greece (331 BC–168 BC)
- Indescribable Beast—Rome (168 BC–AD 476)
- Little Horn—Papal Rome (538–1798)
- Court Sat—Judgment (1844–present)

Creation, in the context of the great controversy, is the overall concept that forms the basis of the vision. This is the great controversy drama through history, discovered by William Miller link by link, that brings us from Daniel's time to the present, forming definite, fixed, immovable landmarks for the historicist student of prophecy. This was the truth proclaimed by Miller, with the contribution of 1844 and the judgment by Seventh-day Adventism. That which was truth then remains truth today.

Question: We know creation is the context of the vision. Since Creation has seven parts, then shouldn't the vision, in harmony with the context, have seven parts? We can see that our historical understanding has clearly delineated only six parts in the vision. There is no seventh part of the vision in our historical perspective. This anomaly is peculiar because, as anyone who is familiar with creation knows, the seventh part is the climax and completion of the process of Creation. The seventh part is the most important part because in it, the Creator is exalted and worshiped above His creation by his creatures, addressing the issue at the heart of the controversy over who is great.

Is there a seventh part of the vision? We don't know. It makes sense that there should be, but how do we objectively identify it from within the text? Let's go back to what we know.

Creation is the context. The reference to night, winds, and water directed our attention to the Creation account in Genesis 1 as the foundation of the vision. Could there be additional connections between this and the vision of Daniel 7 that will objectively give us more insight into the parts of the vision? Let's go to Genesis 1 and look at the process of creation. Is there any basic pattern?

The Creation of this earth took place in seven days. The following is a shortened summary of what was brought into existence in relation to the days:

- Day One—"Let there be light" (Gen. 1:3)
- Day Two—"Let there be a firmament in the midst of the waters, and let it divide the waters from the waters … And God called the firmament Heaven" (vs. 6, 8)
- Day Three—"Let the waters under the heaven be gathered together unto one place, and let the dry land appear" (v. 9)
- Day Four—"Let there be lights in the firmament of the heaven" (v. 14)
- Day Five—"Let the waters bring forth abundantly the moving creature that hath life, and fowl that may fly above the earth in the open firmament of heaven" (v. 20)
- Day Six—"Let the earth bring forth living creatures after his kind … Let us make man in our image, after our likeness: and let them have dominion" (vs. 24, 26).
- Day Seven—"He rested on the seventh day from all his work which he had made. And God blessed the seventh day and sanctified it" (2:2, 3).

There is much that can be said about Creation week, but notice a simple pattern does emerge when we look at the process. The environs that the Creator calls into existence on the first three days—light; separating the waters for the heavens; and land—He then respectively fills on the next set of three days—sun, moon, and stars; birds and fish; and animals and mankind. This simple pattern has been recognized by scholars and laypeople for years. The Creator forms it, then fills it. The relationship of the first set of three days to the second set of three days becomes obvious. The chart below demonstrates the relationship:

A—Day One: "Let there be light"
    B—Day Two: "Let there be a firmament [heaven] in the midst of the waters"
        C—Day Three: "Let the waters be gathered and let dry ground appear"
A'—Day Four: "Let there be lights in the firmament" (sun, moon and stars)
    B'—Day Five: "Let the waters abound … Let the birds fly across the face of the firmament"
        C'—Day Six: "Let the earth bring forth living creatures … let us make man"

The seventh day, the Sabbath, is the climactic, crowning event of Creation week, when all creation acknowledges that its existence and harmony is a result of the goodness of the Creator.

This is obviously not an exhaustive study of the Creation account in Genesis 1, but this observation has supplied us with a simple pattern. A simple three-three-one pattern is easily identified in the Creation account that forms a framework in which the process occurs. Does the vision given to Daniel in chapter 7 have a similar pattern that can be simply identified?

Although we suspect there is a seventh part of the vision from the creation context, we don't know for sure if there is, where it is, or even how it can be identified. However, we do know, or at least we have claimed to know, what the first six parts of the vision are. If there is a pattern in the vision, we should be able to identify it from the first six parts. The pattern itself will identify if there is a seventh part, and if so, what it is. All we need to do is examine the six parts of the vision we do know to see if there is any such pattern or not.

Examining the vision carefully, we realize that all the parts are introduced by some version of Daniel seeing: he looked, saw, or beheld. When looking closer at the phrases for "seeing" that introduces the parts of the vision, a pattern emerges. The following is a simple breakdown of the phrases that identify the parts:

- "I saw in my vision by night, and, behold" (v. 2)
- "And behold" (v. 5)
- "I beheld" (v. 6)
- "I saw in the night visions, and behold" (v. 7)
- "and behold" (v. 8)
- "I beheld" (v. 9)

No matter what version you have, there is the same pattern. Even in those versions that have dropped the "seeing" phrase to introduce the second and fifth part, like the NIV shown below, the translators were at least consistent in retaining a pattern sequence.

- "In my vision at night I looked" (v. 2)—Lion
- "there before me was" (v. 5)—Bear
- "I looked" (v. 6)—Leopard
- "In my vision at night I looked" (v. 7)—Fourth Beast
- "there before me was" (v. 8)—Little Horn
- "I looked" (v. 9)—Judgment

The NASB:

- "I was looking in my vision by night and behold" (v. 2)
- "And behold" (v. 5)
- "I kept looking" (v. 6)
- "I kept looking in the night visions and behold" (v. 7)
- "behold" (v. 8)
- "I kept looking" (v. 9)

In each case, we can plainly see a three-three pattern that consistently repeats the various phrase forms of Daniel seeing. The pattern in chapter 7 does parallel that in Genesis 1. In both patterns, the first and fourth, second and fifth, and third and sixth parts are paired.

Daniel 7
1. "I saw in my vision by night and behold"
   2. "And Behold"
      3. "I beheld"
4. "I saw in the night visions and behold"
   5. "And Behold"
      6. "I beheld"

Genesis 1
1. *Day 1*: Light
   2. *Day 2*: Firmaments
      3. *Day 3*: Dry Land
4. *Day 4*: Sun/Moon/Stars
   5. *Day 5*: Birds/Fish
      6. *Day 6*: Animals/Mankind[33]

This evidence gives us further contextual proof that Creation is the motif behind the vision of Daniel 7. To the point at hand, the discovery of the pattern gives us a template with which to objectively identify the parts of the vision without being accused of forcing our own ideas into the text. If there is a seventh part, then it will fit into the pattern and be easily identified.

According to the pattern, to locate the seventh part of the vision, we simply have to look for the phrase "I saw in the night visions, and behold." The phrase should appear somewhere after verse 9. This will be the introduction of the seventh part of the vision. This seventh part should complete the vision, resolving the conflict between creatures and their Creator over who is great.

The phrase "I saw in the night visions, and behold" does appear after verse 9 and is located in verse 13. The vision of Daniel 7 follows the same three-three-one pattern of the Creation account in Genesis 1. The complete pattern in Daniel 7 looks like this:

Daniel 7
1. "I saw in my vision by night" (v. 2)
   2. "Behold" (v. 5)
      3. "I beheld" (v. 6)
4. "I saw in the night visions" (v. 7)
   5. "Behold" (v. 8)
      6. "I beheld" (v. 9)
7. "I saw in the night visions" (v. 13)

1. *Lion:* 605 BC–539 BC
2. *Bear:* 539 BC–331 BC
3. *Leopard:* 331 BC–168 BC
4. *Incredible Beast:* 168 BC–AD 476
5. *Little Horn:* AD 538–1798
6. *Judgment:* 1844–Today
7. ???

---

[33]The Sabbath is about the Creator. The Sabbath is paired with the first day/light because God is Light (see 1 John 1:5) and the sun, moon, and stars because they were given to "rule the day and the night" (Gen. 1:16), reflecting the rule of the Creator over all creation, which is celebrated by the Sabbath.

According to the Genesis pattern, seven is the completion of the creation process. Thus, in Daniel's vision, the grand climax, the theme of the entire vision, will be the seventh part. The final movement from the sixth scene of the heavenly judgment to the seventh, climactic part contained in verses 13 and 14 will be the final step in the process that completes the great controversy drama. This event will be the present-truth message for God's people who are called to prepare the way for the Creator, inviting all to worship Him. What is this grand and glorious event that moves this prophecy from history into present truth and future glory? We need to survey the pattern of the larger text, then focus on verses 13 and 14:

> **I saw* in my vision by night, and, behold,** the four winds of the heaven strove upon the great sea. And four great beasts came up from the sea, diverse one from another. The **first** *was* like **a lion,** and had eagle's wings: **I beheld*** till the wings thereof were plucked, and it was <u>lifted up</u> from the earth, and made <u>to stand</u> upon the feet as a man, and a man's heart was given to it.
>
> **And behold** another beast, a **second,** like to **a bear,** and it <u>raised up</u> itself on one side, and *it had* three ribs in the mouth of it between the teeth of it: and they said thus unto it, <u>Arise</u>, devour much flesh. After this
>
> **I beheld*,** and lo another, like **a leopard,** which had upon the back of it four wings of a fowl; the beast had also four <u>heads;</u> and <u>dominion</u> was given to it. After this
>
> **I saw* in the night visions, and behold a fourth beast,** dreadful and terrible, and strong exceedingly; and it had <u>great</u> iron teeth: it devoured and brake in pieces, and stamped the residue with the feet of it: and it *was* diverse from all the beasts that *were* before it; and it had ten <u>horns.</u> I considered* the horns,
>
> **and, behold,** there <u>came up</u> among them another **little <u>horn,</u>** before whom there were three of the first horns plucked up by the roots: and, behold, in this horn *were* eyes like the eyes of man, and a mouth speaking great things.
>
> **I beheld*** till the thrones were cast down, and the Ancient of days did sit, whose garment *was* white as snow, and the hair of his head like the pure wool: his throne *was like* the fiery flame, *and* his wheels *as*

burning fire. A fiery stream issued and came forth from before him: thousand thousands ministered unto him, and ten thousand times ten thousand stood before him: **the judgment was set, and the books were opened.** I beheld* then because of the voice of the <u>great</u> words which the horn spake: I beheld* *even* till the beast was slain, and his body destroyed, and given to the burning flame. As concerning the rest of the beasts, they had their <u>dominion</u> taken away: yet their lives were prolonged for a season and time.

I saw* in the night visions, and, behold, *one* like the Son of man came with the clouds of heaven, and came to the Ancient of days, and they brought him near before him. And there was given him dominion, and glory, and a kingdom, that all people, nations, and languages, should serve him: his dominion *is* an everlasting dominion which shall not pass away, and his *kingdom that* which shall not be destroyed. (Daniel 7:2–14, KJV, bold, underline, and asterisk emphases supplied)

"The Son of man" is Jesus. This is the title He used to refer to himself (see Matt. 8:20; 9:6; 10:23; 11:19; 12:8; 16:13; 18:11). The Son of man takes center stage as the heart and focal point in the final act of the drama of the great controversy. The prophecy moves our gaze from the earthly, the beastly, and fixes our attention upon the glorious, the heavenly—upon Jesus. Jesus is the one we need to behold. He is the one we are to proclaim. He is the message; not the antichrist, not the mark of the beast, nor the Sunday laws, or any other creature-manufactured thing. Jesus is the revelation of God to humanity, the source of our salvation. He is the "Alpha and Omega' (Rev. 1:8), the "ruler of God's creation" (3:14, NIV). Jesus is to take center stage in our discussions about the end.

> *Jesus is the one we need to behold. He is the one we are to proclaim. He is the message; not the antichrist, not the mark of the beast, nor the Sunday laws, or any other creature-manufactured thing.*

In the context of the vision, the phrase "Son of man" has more significance when compared with the other players in the drama. In contrast with the beasts and little horn in the earlier parts of the vision, which have some human attributes (see Dan. 7:4, 8), the Son of man is completely human. The beast-to-human analogy of the vision is symbolic of the contrast of the creature-to-Creator concept. Human attributes in the vision symbolize divine qualities. This is fitting symbolism since mankind was created in God's image. Animal characteristics represent creature ideas or concepts of order that are not comprehensive, but rather exploitive and destructive. The beasts—claiming greatness, taking kingly authority to themselves, and rising out the sea—are creatures aspiring to be God. The lion and little horn are presented as creatures that have some human qualities. The lion has the heart of a man (see v. 4), and the little horn has the eyes of a man and a mouth that speaks boastfully (see v. 8).

In contrast to the creatures with some human qualities, the Son of man is completely human. He does not possess some human characteristics, representing divine qualities functioning in partiality, exploiting to exalt self like the little horn does. The Son of man is completely human and therefore a perfect and complete revelation of God to humanity, as well as a perfect and complete Savior of humanity.

Like creation, the importance of the concept of completion is reinforced by the number "7." The seventh part of Daniel 7 contains seven references to the Son of man. Seven, which signifies completeness, manifests on three levels. The references are identified below:

> I saw in the night visions, and, behold, <u>one</u> like the <u>Son of man</u> came with the clouds of heaven, and came to the Ancient of Days, and they brought <u>him</u> near before him. And there was given <u>him</u> dominion, and glory, and a kingdom, that all the people, nations, and languages, should serve <u>him</u>: <u>his</u> dominion is an everlasting dominion, which shall not pass away, and <u>his</u> kingdom that which shall not be destroyed. (Daniel 7:13, 14, underlines supplied).

The symbolism of perfection or completeness in reference to the Son of man has profound implications. Whatever the event is that is typified in the seventh part of the vision will not only complete the salvation ministration through Christ, but will bring humanity to completion in Christ and bring to close the controversy over who is great.

The promise in Scripture that Jesus "must remain in heaven until the universal restoration" (Acts 3:21, NRSV) will then be fulfilled. As humanity is restored to completeness in Christ, so now all the sons and daughters of Adam who accept the invitation to restoration will be brought to completeness to reflect the "image and likeness" (Gen. 1:26) of their Creator. This is the answer to the mystery of how sinful creatures will come to the place and time when the character of God will be "perfectly reproduced in his people."[34]

"God has adopted human nature in the person of His Son, and has carried the same into the highest heaven. It is the 'Son of man' who shares the throne of the universe. ... In Christ the family of earth and the family of heaven are bound together. Christ glorified is our brother. Heaven is enshrined in humanity, and humanity is enfolded in the bosom of Infinite Love."[35] The completed, numbered group (144,000) will follow the Lamb wherever He goes. Where is He going? What is the great event that will bring to completeness Christ's work of salvation? "I saw in the night visions, and, behold, one like the Son of man came with the clouds of heaven, and came to the Ancient of Days, and they brought him near before him" (Dan. 7:13).

Jesus rides a cloud chariot, but this is not the second coming. He "came with the clouds of heaven, and came to the Ancient of Days, and they brought him near before him." Three times the Son of man is described as moving.

The first time, He comes with clouds. Psalm 68:4 tells us to "extol Him who rides the clouds" (NKJV). The psalmist went on to declare that "The chariots of God are twenty thousand, even thousands of angels" (v. 17). The cloud chariot of angels reminds us of the throne chariot in Ezekiel's vision. When Isaiah described Lucifer's desire to exalt himself to the throne of God (see Isa. 14:13), he paralleled the throne with the phrase "I will ascend above the heights of the clouds" (v. 14). The clouds are paralleled with the throne. The Son of man coming with the clouds is a reference to His being exalted to the throne.

Second, He came to the Ancient of Days, and finally "they brought him near before him." The Son of man is being led into the presence of the Father. A special event is about to unfold. "And there was given him dominion, and glory, and a kingdom" (Dan. 7:14a).

The Son of man is "led" (v. 13, NIV) into the presence of the Ancient of Days and "was given ... ." This description stands in contrast to the

---
[34]Ellen White, Christ's Object Lessons (Washington, DC: Review and Herald Publishing Association, 1900), p. 69.
[35]Ellen White, The Desire of Ages (Mountain View, CA: Pacific Press Publishing Association, 1898), pp. 25, 26.

predacious beasts in the vision that are exalting themselves. It is obvious that the kingship is the position in dispute, but the manner in which this authority is obtained reveals the character and essence of the One who receives it. "The kingdom of Satan is a kingdom of force; every individual regards every other as an obstacle in the way of his own advancement, or a steppingstone on which he himself may climb to a higher place."[36]

In contrast, the characteristics of the Son of man are evidence of His qualifications to receive such authority. He is "led into his presence" and "given" (NIV) authority. This is a description of the meek and lowly One who humbles Himself to the will of His Father. The Son of man stands in stark contrast to the ravaging beasts of the sea that exert their will to take by force what is not rightfully theirs. For them, "dominion becomes the prize of the strongest."[37] The Ancient of Days exalts the Son of man because he "bears the glory" (Zech. 6:13), reflects the beauty, and reveals the character of the Eternal One. "Blessed are the meek: for they shall inherit the earth" (Matt. 5:5).

As the Son of man's movement is described in three ways, so He was given three things: "dominion, and glory, and a kingdom." The coronation scene in 2 Kings provides us with the biblical background to interpret the symbols. The coronation of Joash as king is important because it is not an isolated incident but rather described as happening "according to the custom" (2 Kings 11:14, NKJV). This is the traditional, liturgical procedure for the coronation of a king in Israel. "And he brought out the king's son, put the crown on him, and *gave him* the Testimony; they made him king and anointed him, and they clapped their hands and said, 'Long live the king!'" (v. 12, NKJV).

First, the king's son is described as being brought, the same as the Son of man being brought (see Dan. 7:13), which again emphasizes humility—a servant's heart. At his coronation, the king is given three emblems: the crown, the Testimony or scroll of the Law, and an anointing. These three emblems that the king literally received in ancient times are types of the three emblems given to the Son of man, the true King, at His coronation. "And to him was given dominion, and glory, and a kingdom" (v. 14).

The covenant scroll or copy of the Law received by earthly kings is an emblem of the dominion to be received by Christ because the earthly kings were to rule according to the laws written in the scroll:

---

[36]Ellen G. White, The Desire of Ages (Mountain View, CA: Pacific Press Publishing Association, 1898), p. 436.
[37]Ibid.

> Also it shall be, when he sits on the throne of his kingdom, that he shall write for himself a copy of this law in a book, from *the one* before the priests, the Levites. And it shall be with him, and he shall read it all the days of his life, that he may learn to fear the LORD his God and be careful to observe all the words of this law and these statutes, that his heart may not be lifted above his brethren, that he may not turn aside from the commandment *to* the right hand or *to* the left, and that he may prolong *his* days in his kingdom, he and his children in the midst of Israel. (Deuteronomy 17:18–20, NKJV)

The king was not to make up his own laws, but execute the Law of God. This was God's directive to Israel regarding the kingship. In this way, the scroll of the Law is an emblem of dominion.

The king was anointed with a "horn of oil" (1 Sam. 16:13; 1 Kings 1:39). This is one of the reasons that the Messiah, the anointed One, is called a Horn (1 Sam. 2:10; 2 Sam. 22:3; Ps. 89:17; 132:17; Luke 1:69). This is why the antichrist figure of Daniel 7 and 8 is described as a little horn or false messiah. The anointing of the earthly king is a type of the glory that the true King will receive. Jesus will be anointed by the Holy Spirit as King, just as He was anointed at His baptism, Pentecost, and other phases of His salvation ministry. The anointing of Christ as King by the Holy Spirit will empower the church to truly reflect the glory of the Father. The anointing oil is an emblem of the King's glory.

The crown of the earthly king is the emblem of kingship that the true King will receive. The word "crown" comes from the Latin word *corona* and symbolizes the shafts of light that stream forth from the king, who is the personification of the sun (see Ps. 132:17, 18). However, Jesus is the true "Sun of Righteousness" that rises with healing in His wings (Mal. 4:2). Perhaps the crown of Jesus will be living light that shines from His inherent divinity and flashes through His nail-pierced brow, an extension of the concept presented in Habakkuk 3:4. Whatever form the crown takes, it encompasses the concept of kingship. The three emblems that earthly kings received at their coronation (see 2 Kings 11:12) are types of the antitypical heavenly emblems—"dominion, glory and kingship"—received by the Son of man in Daniel 7.

- Dominion—Copy of the Law
- Glory—Anointing
- Kingship—Crown

As if it is not compelling enough that the seventh part of Daniel 7 brings to light the same Christ event that Zachariah envisioned—the coronation of Jesus as King of kings, in harmony with Zachariah's coming out from Babylon (see Zech. 6:10), Jeremiah's bringing "up from the North country" (Jer. 23:8), and Isaiah's "recovering" where "the gentiles seek Him" (Isa. 11:10, 11)—Daniel 7:13, 14 also describes a worldwide movement on the earth that corresponds to and is a result of this movement in heaven. The message to serve Him goes to "all the people, nations, and languages" (Dan. 7:14).

The three stages or groups of people are a common, ancient Eastern cultural description of the whole kingdom. The three categories or groups include everyone within the kingdom and also describe the process in which a proclamation or decree of the king would go forth over his domain.

In Daniel 3, when all the kingdom of Babylon is commanded by royal decree to fall down and worship the golden image, the kingdom is described in this same three-part phrase: "people, nations, and languages" (vs. 4, 7, 29). Again, in chapter four, when King Nebuchadnezzar wrote an account of his experience with God and sent it forth as a royal decree, he described his domain as "all the earth," defined in the same three-part language: "all people, nations, and languages" (v. 1). Daniel described to Belshazzar the kingdom of his father in the same way: "for the majesty that he gave him, all people, nations, and languages, trembled and feared before him" (5:19). King Darius wrote his royal decree in the same way (see 6:25). The repetition demonstrates how commonplace this imagery was, and the fact that the Babylonians as well as the Medes and Persians used the same imagery is evidence of this.

The kingdom that the Son of man receives is all-inclusive and described in this ancient kingdom language of "people, nations and languages." The contextual evidence in the historical chapters of Daniel, describing royal proclamations or decrees going forth in a specific order, gives insight into the process of the heavenly King's decree that "all people, nations and languages should serve him" (7:14). This is a royal decree that goes forth to the three stages of the newly installed King's domain, inviting everyone to worship, serve, and become a subject of the King. This is the technical aspect of what we call the three angels' messages.

The movement on the earth being described in this three-stage, royal proclamation inviting all to serve the Son may give us a clue as to why the vision mentions three times the movement of the Son to receive His kingdom. Recall that the "Son of man came with the clouds of heaven, and came to the Ancient of days, and they brought Him near before him" (v. 13). It just may be that the connections between the movements of Christ in heaven and the movements of His church on earth are more intimate than we have understood.

It's impossible to be concrete that the triple mention of His movement in heaven is connected to the three-stage movement on earth. However, the repetition of the threes and sevens in this passage are completely in harmony with the series of threes and sevens that later characterize the book of Revelation. It is possible that the repetition of His coming is described as occurring in three phases because it correctly reflects the three stages of the decree that make the earth the domain of the newly installed King.

The "people" represent the first group. They are people because they are from the culture of the King. They are covenant people, closest to the king because of their common knowledge and background. They would be the first to receive the decree to worship. The "nations" represent other civilized peoples. Familiar with the covenant people, they have become part of the covenant community through invitation rather than by birth. They would receive the news and invitation to worship next. Finally, languages represent all others, usually considered barbaric because their language and customs are so different from the ruling class. This was the mindset that formed the imagery of the three-stage decree that went forth in ancient kingdoms.

> *Not only does the overall movement of Jesus becoming King in heaven correspond to a great revival movement on earth, but it repeats the Millerite movement in that it "prophesies again" the first angel's message.*

Not only does the overall movement of Jesus becoming King in heaven correspond to a great revival movement on earth, but it repeats the Millerite movement in that it "prophesies again" the first angel's message. "His dominion is an everlasting dominion, which shall not pass away, and his kingdom that which shall not be destroyed" (v. 14c)

Christ's dominion and kingship are described in harmony with the divine, everlasting nature of the Ancient of days. The three stages of the eternal gospel going forth in Daniel 7:13–14 to all people, nations, and languages is the same eternal gospel given by the three angels' messages in Revelation 14:6–12—the final invitation to serve/worship the King and partake in His everlasting kingdom. This proclamation will be the fullness of which 1844 was a forerunner. Mrs. White spoke frankly about the future proclamation of the three angels:

> The first and second messages were given in 1843 and 1844, and we are now under the proclamation of the third; but all three of the messages are still to be proclaimed. It is just as essential now as ever before that they shall be repeated to those who are seeking for the truth. By pen and voice we are to sound the proclamation, showing their order, and the application of the prophecies that bring us to the third angel's message. There cannot be a third without the first and the second. These messages we are to give to the world in publications, in discourses, showing in the line of prophetic history the things that have been and the things that will be.[38]

The seventh part of the vision of Daniel 7 moves us from historical prophecy into present truth, "the things which shall be hereafter" (Rev. 1:19). This is compelling evidence that the vision of the event of Jesus becoming King in Zechariah is no coincidence. The seventh part of the prophecy of Daniel 7 also presents the installation of Christ as King as the next event to be proclaimed to the world. Jesus, now our High Priest in heaven, is to be installed as the King of kings. Before Jesus can come as King, he must *become* King.

This event in heaven will be accompanied by a great movement here on earth. The eternal gospel, the first angel's message, will be proclaimed to "all people, nations and languages," that all "should serve Him" (Dan. 7:14). Or, in the language of Zachariah, all will be invited to the marriage supper of the Lamb. "Everyone will invite his neighbor Under His vine and under His fig tree" (Zech. 3:10, NKJV). The wise will awaken to the marriage feasts and heed the call.

The King is becoming!

---

[38] Ellen G. White, Selected Messages, book 2 (Washington, DC: Review and Herald Publishing Association, 1958), pp. 104, 105.

Chapter 5

The Stone Becomes a Mountain

The accuracy of our study of Daniel 7 can be affirmed in the corresponding prophecy of Daniel 2. The parallelism of the two prophecies forms the structure upon which the Adventist historicist understanding of prophecy is built. Uriah Smith wrote, "The image of chapter 2 is exactly with the vision of the four beasts of chapter 7."[39] For further confirmation, "The prophecy of ch. 7 covers essentially the same span of history as the dream of ch. 2, both reaching from the prophet's day to the time of the establishment of the kingdom of God."[40]

This template gives us an objective means to examine our conclusions from Daniel 7. If what has been presented from this chapter is established by the parallel prophecy of Daniel 2, the weight of the combined evidence would be forceful enough to remove any question as to the soundness of the interpretation. The harmony of the two prophesies, presenting

---

[39]Uriah Smith, Daniel and the Revelation (Nashville, TN: Southern Publishing Association, 1949), p. 66.
[40]The Seventh-day Adventist Bible Commentary, vol. 4, ed. F.D. Nichol (Washington, DC: Review and Herald Publishing Association, 1954), p. 819.

parallel descriptions of the kingdoms of the world from Babylon down through history, is reflected below:

Daniel 2	Interpretation	Daniel 7
Gold	Babylon	Lion
Silver	Medo-Persia	Bear
Bronze	Greece	Leopard
Iron	Rome	Dragon
Iron-Clay/Ten Toes	Ten Kingdoms/Papal Rome	Ten Horns/Little Horn

The parallelism is evident in the step-by-step harmony of the earthly kingdoms. The detail of the metals, aligned with the kingdoms they represent and the matching beasts, reveals a simplicity that is profound. The accuracy of the prophecies is evidence of the fingerprint of God.

Our historical understanding of Nebuchadnezzar's dream of the rise and fall of kingdoms is rock solid. Our view of history is crystal clear and spot on. Our understanding of the end is where our vision gets cloudy. When we go beyond the earthy kingdoms of Daniel 2 and focus our attention on the end of the prophecy, the principle of the parallelism of the prophecies as a means of affirming our understanding of the worldly kingdoms is suddenly abandoned. This is significant because if parallelism is the hermeneutical principle by which we interpret the prophecies of Daniel 2 and 7, then the principle must apply to the whole prophecy. One cannot apply a so-called principle to only certain aspects of the prophecy and then discard it partway through it. It then ceases to be a principle. What's the dilemma?

Uriah Smith wrote that the stone that strikes the feet of the statue is the second coming of Christ.[41] Roy Allen Anderson[42] as well as other Adventist writers, following Smith's lead, have made this almost standard Adventist teaching. This traditional position presented no harm, and when questioned about not comparing with Daniel 7, the explanation went something like this: "The prophecy of the image is more general and doesn't have the same details of Daniel 7." The issue never became serious enough to be addressed, so the idea stuck, and the contradiction with the hermeneutic of parallelism stayed with us.

---

[41] Uriah Smith, Daniel and the Revelation (Nashville, TN: Southern Publishing Association, 1949), p. 79.
[42] Roy Allen Anderson, Unfolding Daniel's Prophecies (Nampa, ID: Pacific Press, 1975), p. 57.

Daniel 2	Interpretation	Daniel 7
Gold	Babylon	Lion
Silver	Medo-Persia	Bear
Bronze	Greece	Leopard
Iron	Rome	Dragon
Iron-Clay/Ten toes	Ten Kingdoms/Papal Rome	Ten Horns/Little Horn
The Stone	?	Court sat—1844

Like Daniel 7, our understanding of the end of chapter 2 has been generalized under the umbrella of the second coming. There seemed to be no need for an understanding of a specific process, or that there even was a process, in the formation of the kingdom of God. The passing of time and the current confusion about last-day events is evidence that the coming of God's kingdom is not as simple as saying, "Jesus is coming back." The longer we are here and the end has not come, the more compelling is the evidence that our understanding of the end has been shortsighted and oversimplified.

There is a credible need for an understanding of the end that is before us if we are to intelligently act as players in the process. Besides, accepting the idea that God left out the whole judgment process in the prophecy of the image of Daniel 2 and jumped to the second coming sounds suspicious to me in light of the importance of the judgment highlighted throughout the rest of the book. Let's take a look: Is the stone of Daniel 2 that strikes the image a symbol of the second coming, as Uriah Smith suggested, or does the principle of parallelism apply?

> *The passing of time and the current confusion about last-day events is evidence that the coming of God's kingdom is not as simple as saying, "Jesus is coming back." The longer we are here and the end has not come, the more compelling is the evidence that our understanding of the end has been shortsighted and oversimplified.*

The hermeneutic of biblical parallelism between the two prophecies is established by the shared content, context, and structure of the prophecies. We know well the parallel content: the descriptions of the earthly kingdoms from Babylon down to the end.

The context of the two prophecies is also parallel. King Nebuchadnezzar has a dream about a "great statue" (2:31) in conflict with a "great mountain" (v. 35). This controversy over who is great reflects the same struggle we saw in Daniel 7, where the "great" sea (7:2) and "great" beasts (v. 3) are in conflict with the four winds of heaven. The great controversy, or the controversy over who is great, is the context of both prophecies.

The structure of Nebuchadnezzar's dream parallels that of Daniel's vision. The structure, according to Daniel's explanation (Dan. 2:31–35) is:

"You were looking O king and there was a *great* statue" (v. 31, emphasis added)

1. Head of gold
2. Chest and arms of silver
3. Middle and thighs of bronze
4. Legs of iron
5. Feet partly of Iron and partly Clay

"As you looked on" (v. 34)

6. Stone cut out of the mountain but not by human hands
7. Stone becomes a "great" mountain and fills the whole earth

The structure above contains a distinct division, as emphasized in the format presented. The first five parts take place on the earth and describe the actions of the kingdoms of humanity. The sixth and seventh parts describe God's actions in heaven and the establishment of the everlasting kingdom of the Most High.

Daniel 7 follows the same distinctive pattern. The first five parts of the vision describe the human kingdoms of earth: the lion, bear, leopard, "dragon," and little horn. The sixth and seventh parts symbolize what takes place in heaven: "thrones are set in place, the court is set, the books are opened," and then the inauguration of the King. Both prophecies record the five-step degradation of humanity that culminates in the abomination of desolation—mankind exalting itself as God, in conflict with the final saving acts of the Creator.

The parallelism of Daniel 2 and 7 is also evident in that their components are introduced by some form of looking. In Daniel 2, each section of the explanation of the dream is introduced with the phrase, "you were looking" (v. 31, 34, etc.), while in chapter 7, as we noted, each of the specific parts are identified by a form of seeing.

From this structure, we also recognize that both prophecies have seven parts. This means that all the symbolism of creation, in the context of the great controversy that we saw in Daniel 7, also applies to the process described here in chapter 2. The intricacy of the shared content, context, and structure of the two prophecies establishes a sound platform for us to confidently stand behind the hermeneutic of biblical parallelism. The two prophecies are describing the same process with alternate symbols; each confirms the accuracy of the other in their description of the great controversy.

The scriptural evidence, validating the hermeneutic of biblical parallelism between the two prophecies, means that the stone imagery of Daniel 2 must be an alternative symbol of the judgment of 7:9–12 and cannot be the second coming, as some have suggested. It's significant that there is no support in Mrs. White's writings for Uriah Smith's interpretation of the stone as the second coming. This lack of support gives sound footing to at least seriously consider what is being presented.

Questions that need biblical answers immediately come to mind. How do the symbols of the two prophecies harmonize to describe the same process? Specifically, how does the stone in Daniel 2 symbolize the judgment of Daniel 7, instead of the second coming?

To answer this question, we need to understand the imagery around the symbol of the stone in the context of the vision. Then, to make sure we aren't pressing our ideas into the text, we must compare our conclusions about the stone with other biblical usages of the symbol. Through this process, we can identify the stone symbolism in the sixth part of Daniel 2 and objectively compare it with "the throne, the court seated, and the books opened" symbolism in the sixth part of Daniel 7.

> As you looked on, a stone was cut out, not by human hands, and it struck the statue on its feet of iron and clay and broke them in pieces. Then the iron, the clay, the bronze, the silver, and the gold, were all broken in pieces and became like the chaff of the summer threshing floors; and the wind carried them away, so that not a trace of them could be found. (Daniel 2:34, 35, NRSV).

The sixth part of Nebuchadnezzar's dream features a stone, clearly the most dramatic event of the prophecy so far. The rock reveals the fundamental principles of the conflict by contrast with the elements that comprise the statue. All the elements are similar in that they are natural, created by God. However, the elements that make up the statue have been refined, processed, and shaped by "human hands" into a component of an image that reflects mankind's desire to exalt and glorify self. Mankind forms a god in its own image and fashions its concepts of reality, labeled truth, around this false self.

All that fallen humanity deems as significant is blended together in the image. The statue represents and reflects mankind's technological abilities to conform its environs around itself and reinforces the lie that a creature is god. The idol, formed in mankind's image, is a fit representation of its rebellion against its Creator. The maturing of the great controversy is depicted as an idol in the form of a man being set up as God—the abomination that makes desolate.

The stone, in contrast, is specifically described as being "cut out, not by human hands" (v. 34). The phrase "not by human hands" reveals a totally different refining and shaping process, resulting in a standard and process ordained by the Creator that reflects His image and likeness. The light of this truth immediately reveals the futility of mankind in its attempts to be God, twisting its concepts of reality around itself in its attempts to justify itself. The stone imagery therefore not only describes the judgment by revealing the motive behind the image, but it becomes the standard to which all are compared in the judgment.

The stone as the basis of the judgment in Daniel 2 is very specific. The stone is "cut" (v. 34), which prefigures the "cutting off" of the Messiah to be presented later in 9:26. This scriptural allusion to the death of Christ for the salvation of all who will believe forms the basis of the judgment. The self-sacrificing love of God, His essence, is the standard in the judgment that exposes the selfish, exploitive desire in humans to exalt themselves through the works of their hands, which comprise the statue. The cutting of the rock as a symbol of the death of the Messiah that gives life to the world is common, biblical imagery.

In Exodus 17, Moses is commanded to smite the rock so that lifegiving water will flow to the thirsty multitude. In Zechariah 3:9, the Lord presents to Joshua a stone with seven eyes in which He will "engrave an inscription" and "remove the sin of this land in a single day" (NIV). The cut stone throughout Scripture represents the death of our Creator for the salvation of humanity. It is clear that Jesus is "that Rock" (1 Cor. 10:4) that is smitten to give living water to the thirsty. The self-sacrificing love of God, as revealed through Christ on the cross, is the rock on which He has established His everlasting kingdom.

The stone set in contrast with the image illuminates the vision, shining great light upon us about the judgment. "Not by human hands" (Dan. 2:34, NRSV) means that only the selfless works of love can pass through the stream of fire that flows from His throne and still exist. The judgment is a time when the revelation of God and the means He has provided for the salvation of humanity are set in contrast to the futility of the works of mankind's hands, revealing its inability to save itself. This flood of light tests the foundation upon which every person has built his or her house. According to Jesus (see Matt. 7:24), those who built on the rock are secure; those who build on the sand will be, like the statue, crushed and swept away by the winds. This appeal of Christ to the people of His day is the same message of judgment that exposes and destroys the image in the end.

Is it a biblical concept that the stone or rock symbolism is intimately tied to judgment? Again, the Scriptures declare, "at the mouth of two witnesses, or at the mouth of three witnesses, shall the matter be established" (Deut. 19:15).

The first testimony to establish the biblical connection of the rock or stone to the concept of judgement is in Deuteronomy 32. This occasion is significant because God is calling the people together to witness against them. Moses commands, "Gather unto me all the elders of your tribes, and your officers, that I may speak these words in their ears, and call heaven and earth to record against them. For I know that after my death ye will utterly corrupt yourselves" (31:28, 29, KJV). He begins by calling heaven and earth as witnesses (see 32:1), then says, "Because I will publish the name of the LORD: ascribe ye greatness unto our God. He is the Rock, his work is perfect: for all his ways are judgment: a God of truth and without iniquity, just and right is he" (vs. 3, 4).

God's name, His essence or character, which is "perfect" and "without iniquity," is the standard by which Israel is to be judged. Seven times in this discourse, Moses called God the "Rock": He is the rock that sustained them in the wilderness (see v. 13); "the Rock of his salvation" (v. 15). "the Rock that begat thee" (v. 18): Israel could not be defeated "except their Rock had sold them" (v. 30); regarding the heathen, Moses said, "For their rock is not as our Rock, even our enemies themselves being judges" (v. 31); God's "just and right" character, which is described as a Rock, is what makes manifest that Israel is "a perverse and crooked generation" (v. 5); God "is the Rock, his work is perfect; for all his ways are judgment" (v. 4). The rock as a symbol is directly tied to judgment.

The second witness is found in Isaiah 28. Here, God is again appealing to His people to come out of their deceit because "they also have erred through wine, and through strong drink are out of the way" (v. 7). He calls "the weary to rest; and this is the refreshing; yet they would not hear" (v. 12). In the midst of this warning of "a consumption, even determined upon the whole earth" (v. 22), God gives this appeal. "Therefore thus saith the Lord GOD, Behold, I lay in Zion for a foundation a stone, a tried stone, a precious corner *stone*, a sure foundation: he that believeth shall not make haste. Judgment also will I lay to the line, and righteousness to the plummet; and the hail shall sweep away the refuge of lies" (vs. 16, 17).

The laying of "a foundation stone," with a three-part description of the flawless character thereof this stone—tried, precious, and sure—accompanied by the appeal to believe and so find rest, is paralleled with laying "judgment" to the line and "righteousness to the plummet." The surety and righteousness of the stone is the standard of the judgment and what makes manifest the "refuge of lies," symbolized by wine and strong drink, and sweeps it away. Isaiah, using the same imagery, later says, "Listen to me, you who pursue righteousness and who seek the LORD: Look to the Rock from which you were cut and the quarry from which you were hewn" (51:1, NIV). The Rock, in the context of being cut and hewn, establishes the standard of righteousness. Again, we see the biblical concept of the stone intimately connected with judgment.

The third biblical witness for connecting stone symbolism to the judgment comes from Daniel 7 and the symbols employed to describe the judgment. "I beheld till thrones were cast down, and the Ancient of days did sit" (v. 9). Daniel then describes characteristics of the Ancient of days and His throne. He concludes the section with "the judgment was set, and the books were opened" (v. 10). The character and throne of God is established as the standard and measure by which the judgment takes place.

"The LORD is king; let the peoples tremble! He sits enthroned upon the cherubim; let the earth quake" (Ps. 99:1, NRSV). The ark of the covenant is described as a throne (see 80:1). The ark contained the tablets of the law, the Ten Commandments (see Heb. 9:4). The tables of the law were made by God and given to Moses on Mt. Sinai. "The tablets were the work of God, the writing was the writing of God, graven upon the tablets" (Ex 32:16). They were cut out of the mountain. The words of God were cut into the stone by His finger. They are concrete symbols of a rock cut out the mountain "not by human hands." The tablets of the law and the ark of the covenant in which they rested were not subject to the tampering of human hands, as the story of Uzzah dramatically teaches.

Daniel 7 places the character of God and His throne as the basis for judgment. Within the throne or ark are the two tablets of the Ten Commandments—stones cut out of a mountain by divine hands. These stones of judgment are also set in contrast to "THE MOTHER OF HARLOTS" (Rev. 17:5) by whom "the inhabitants of the earth have been made drunk with the wine of her fornication" (v. 2). These stones of judgment expose the little horn in Daniel 7, who "thinks to change times and laws" (7:25). Again, we see the stone imagery directly connected to judgment, giving solid biblical support for the conclusion that the symbol of the stone cut out of the mountain in the sixth part of Daniel 2 is parallel imagery of and directly connected to the throne and judgment scene in the sixth part of Daniel 7.

This Old Testament imagery of the Rock takes on flesh in the person of Jesus our Lord. He says of Himself, "The stone the builders rejected has become the capstone" (Matt. 21:42, NIV). The capstone is the most significant stone of the temple gate. It was placed above the threshold and formed the porch of the temple, the place of judgment. Jesus claimed this place of supreme authority as his own: "I am the door" (John 10:9). Later, He states more clearly, "I am the way, the truth, and the life: no man cometh unto the Father, but by me" (14:6). A significant connection of the law to the gate is confirmed in Deuteronomy 6:9. Here, Israel is instructed to inscribe the law on the doorposts of the houses and gates. Jesus is the Rock of our salvation (see 1 Cor 10:4), but to the lost, He is "a stone of stumbling, and a rock of offence" (1 Peter 2:8). Thus, Jesus can declare, "the Father judgeth no man, but hath committed all judgment unto the Son" (John 5:22).

Jesus significantly applies the imagery of Daniel 2 in the context of the decision that all must make, and the resulting consequences, to either accept or reject Him. After sharing the parable of the tenants to the religious authorities, who claimed to need no instruction, Jesus makes His most direct biblical reference to the stone smashing the image in Daniel 2: "And he who falls on this stone will be broken to pieces; but on whomever it falls, it will scatter him like dust" (Matt. 21:44, NASB).

He is clearly stating to his hearers that their decision regarding their relationship to the stone will determine their destiny. All who see their need, give up on their ability to save themselves, and come falling on the stone will be broken. This process will result in life. All who refuse to see their need and reject the stone will be crushed to dust. Jesus is the focal point of the judgment. Life and death hang in the balance over one's decision to accept or reject Christ, the Rock of our salvation.

> *All who see their need, give up on their ability to save themselves, and come falling on the stone will be broken. This process will result in life. All who refuse to see their need and reject the stone will be crushed to dust. Jesus is the focal point of the judgment.*

Another significant, New Testament demonstration of the connection of the stone to judgment imagery is when Pilate presides in judgment over Jesus. "He brought Jesus out and sat down on the judge's seat at a place known as the Stone Pavement (which in Aramaic is called Gabbatha)" (John 19:13, NIV). The stone pavement is the judge's seat from which Pilate would declare his verdict. The stone as a symbol of judgment has sound biblical support.

This biblical evidence forms the basis of our conclusion that the judgment passage of Daniel 7:9—"thrones were set in place" (NRSV); "The court was seated, and the books were opened" (NKJV)—parallels "a stone cut out, not by human hands" (2:34, NRSV). The integrity of the principle of biblical parallelism between the prophecies of Daniel 2 and 7 is upheld and affirmed. The stone of chapter 2 is an alternate symbol of the judgment process in chapter 7, not a symbol of the second coming, which would violate the principle biblical of parallelism.

The next phrase in the passage is the "chaff on a threshing floor in the summer" (2:35, NIV). The "threshing floor" phrase as judgment is also well-documented, biblical imagery. In 2 Samuel 24, David numbers Israel. The resulting plague ensues as an angel holding a sword halts at the threshing floor of Araunah the Jebusite. David builds an altar and sacrifices the bullocks to stop the destruction. The stone altar, built by undressed stones (not cut by human hands), and the sacrifice at the threshing floor are describing an actual scene of judgment.

The kingdoms of mankind that set themselves up in opposition to the stone are broken to pieces until they are like chaff on the threshing floor. The stone exposes the basic, elemental principle of the image's existence, and it is revealed as dust. This is fitting imagery. Consider God's decree to people who believe the lie that they are God and trust in the works of their hands for life: "From dust thou art, and unto dust shalt thou return" (Gen. 3:19). The wind carries them away, and not a trace of them is found (see Dan. 2:35). "As *for* man, his days are like grass; As a flower of the field, so he flourishes. For the wind passes over it, and it is gone, And its place remembers it no more. But the mercy of the LORD *is* from everlasting to everlasting On those who fear Him" (Ps 103:15–17, NKJV).

John the Baptist used the threshing floor imagery to describe a judgment process that prepares the way for the coming of the Messiah: "His winnowing fork is in his hand, and he will clear his threshing floor, gathering his wheat into the barn and burning up the chaff with unquenchable fire" (Matt. 3:12, NIV).

The stone cut out of the mountain is not the second coming but the judgment that must take place beforehand. Having established a biblical basis for the parallel between the stone of Daniel 2 and the court judgment concept of Daniel 7, what insight on the judgment does the dream of Daniel 2 provide?

If we build something, we start with the foundation and work up, but the image of Daniel 2 begins at the head and progresses downward. This direction of development is more in line with the Eastern concepts of cycles of kingdoms rather than describing a building process. The beauty and value of the materials decrease during the process until only the raw, plain principles of the image that are its foundation are revealed. Though the facade of beauty is gone at the base, the principle is worldwide in its application and encompasses all the kings of this world (see Dan 2:44). The maturing of the phenomenon of mankind exalting itself and the works of human hands is the fullness of the rejection of the Creator and termed the "abomination of desolation." This description would be readily apparent to any Jew reading Daniel because the setting up of idols is an abomination and strictly forbidden in the Ten Commandments.

These principles unite all the kingdoms of mankind in the end and thus have the strength of iron, but the common theme of self-exaltation, by its very nature, means the unity is fragile and short-lived, represented by the brittle clay. This fragile unity is based on the principle of a common enemy. In this context, the completion of the image is dependent on the revelation of the stone, which is the Prince that reveals the principles of God's kingdom. This light exposes the fallacy of the principles that make up the human kingdoms that comprise the image. With a clear delineation of the issues, all the inhabitants of the earth must decide as to which kingdom they belong. To choose a prince is to choose the principle, and vice versa. This decision-making process is required for the image to be complete. The paradox is that the completion of the image, when it comes to maturity, is its destruction.

Many people struggle with seeing the papacy in the prophecy of Nebuchadnezzar's dream. They go down through the symbols from Babylon to Medo-Persia, Medo-Persia to Greece, and Greece to Rome. Rome is divided into ten parts; the ten horns of Daniel 7:7 fits nicely with the ten toes of 2:42. There seems to be nothing in the prophecy after the ten toes until the cutting out of the rock. This type of linear reasoning is common, and although it has its place in helping to see the timeline of historic kingdoms, it also limits one's understanding of the symbolic imagery employed in the prophecy.

Look again at the introduction of the stone: "You watched while a stone was cut out without hands, which struck the image on its feet of iron and clay, and broke them in pieces. Then the iron, the clay, the bronze, the silver, and the gold were crushed together, and became like chaff from the threshing floors; the wind carried them away so that no trace of them was found" (Dan. 2:34, 35, NIV).

The phrase that lists the materials challenges our linear thinking. We think of Babylon existing, then ending when Medo-Persia arises; Medo-Persia ends when Greece arises, and so on. However, the prophecy doesn't describe it this way. All the kingdoms exist simultaneously and are destroyed at the same time. The image is growing or developing with each new addition. This is the same imagery used in Daniel 7 to describe the four beasts. They exist simultaneously (see vs. 11, 12). Revelation 13 picks up this symbolism to describe the beast from the sea: "The beast which I saw was like unto a leopard, and his feet were as the feet of a bear, and his mouth as the mouth of a lion: and the dragon gave him his power, and his seat, and great authority" (vs. 2, 3). The beast of Revelation 13 is a composite of the beasts of Daniel 7. The kingdoms are not linear, but synchronistic.

The great image of Daniel 2 is developing with each new addition and comes to completion only at the cutting of the rock out of the mountain. The rock cut out by divine hands shines light on the image to not only reveal "the man of lawlessness" (2 Thess. 2:3), but bring it to maturity. The great image is of a man. The exaltation and worship of a man as God becomes apparent when seen in contrast to the stone. At this time, all the religions of the world unite under the philosophy of humanism in the time of the cutting of the rock; thus will be revealed "the man of lawlessness" or "the man of sin" prophesied of in 2 Thessalonians. What we haven't been able to see is right before us. The entirety of the image in its completed form is the fulfilment of mankind's attempt to exalt itself in the place of God—the abomination that causes desolation.

Humanism will unify and synchronize the religions of the world and the kingdoms of the earth together under the papal power during the time of the cutting of the rock. The two events are linked together and happen simultaneously. Only then does the image come to completion, which ironically, will be its destruction.

"But the stone that struck the statue became a great mountain and filled the whole earth" (Dan 2:35, NRSV). The seventh part of the vision of Daniel 2 is the climax of the prophecy, just as the coronation of the Son of man is in Daniel 7. Both scenes describe the end of the controversy over who is great by some curious, cosmic event that centers upon the Son of God. In Daniel 2, the stone that was cut becomes a "great" mountain in contrast to the "great" image. The symbolism corresponds with Daniel 7 in three aspects: 1) the kingship imagery employed to describe the event, 2) the emphasis on the process of becoming King, and 3) the ensuing royal decree that goes forth over all creation, causing all to decide which king they will worship.

The kingship imagery of Daniel 2 revolves around the mountain symbolism. According to Revelation 17, a mountain represents a king. "The seven heads are seven mountains on which the woman sits. They are also seven kings" (vs. 9, 10, NKJV). The stone becoming a great mountain refers to the specific process of Christ's coronation and installation as King on the throne in heaven.

The same king to mountain symbolism is evident in Psalm 48: "like the heights of Zaphon[43] is Mount Zion, the city of the Great King" (v. 2, NIV). Biblical symbolism freely employs a mountain as a symbol of the king and his kingdom. Micah 4 (as well as Isaiah 2) describes God's kingdom as a mountain: "In the last days the mountain of the LORD's temple will be established as the highest of the mountains ... 'In that day,' declares the LORD ... The LORD will rule over them in Mount Zion from that day and forever. ... the former dominion will be restored to you; kingship will come to the Daughter of Jerusalem" (vs. 1, 6, 7, 8, NIV).

---

[43] "Zaphon can refer to a sacred mountain or the direction north" (NIV footnote to Psalm 48:2)

Psalm 2 significantly connects the process of becoming king to a place of authority, a mountain. "I have installed My King Upon Zion, My holy mountain" (v. 6, NASB). The next verse describes the royal decree that goes forth at the installation of the new King. The fact that Psalm 2 describes all three aspects—the King, the process of becoming King, and the resulting decree that goes forth to worship Him—which we identified in Daniel 2:35, is significant because it is a coronation psalm.

The stone becomes a mountain, meaning that Christ has become King, but not just any king; He is described as becoming a "great" mountain. The emphasis upon the concept of "great" throughout the study of Daniel 2 and 7 has been explained in light of the great controversy. Jesus is no ordinary king. He becomes the great King of kings. He settles all questions and answers all objections involved in the great controversy, to close every mouth and silence every tongue.

> *It becomes powerfully clear that what has been generalized in the past as the second coming is actually a detailed description of the process of the installation of Christ as King and the establishment of His kingdom by the decree of worship that goes out to all the earth.*

In harmony with the seven-part structure of Daniel 7, we see that the seventh part of chapter 2 describes the exaltation of the stone to kingship with the terms "great" and "mountain." This stone becomes a great, living mountain that expands until it fills the whole earth. This corresponds with the seventh part of Daniel 7, when the Son of man is installed as King and the decree of His dominion goes out to all people, nations, and languages—the whole earth. This imagery is reflected in Daniel 2 by the stone becoming a living mountain that fills the earth.

It becomes powerfully clear that what has been generalized in the past as the second coming is actually a detailed description of the process of the installation of Christ as King and the establishment of His kingdom by the decree of worship that goes out to all the earth. The kingship of Christ is the great cosmic event that alters the course of time and space, bringing the issues of the controversy to light for every inhabitant of the earth to make an informed decision. "And this gospel of the kingdom shall be preached in all the world for a witness unto all nations; and then shall the end come" (Matt. 24:14, KJV).

The parallel picture of the two prophecies from Daniel's time down to the end looks like this:

Daniel 2	Daniel 7	Interpretation	
Head of gold	Lion	Babylon	605–539 BC
Chest of silver	Bear	Medo-Persia	539–331 BC
Belly of bronze	Leopard	Greece	331–168 BC
Legs of iron	"Dragon"	Rome	168 BC–AD 476
Feet of iron and clay	Little horn	Papal Rome	538–1798
Stone cut out	Court sits	Judgment	1844–Present
Stone becomes a mountain	Son of man's coronation	Kingship	Present truth

The seventh part of the vision of Daniel 2 mirrors the same truth discovered in Daniel 7. This is compelling evidence, harmonizing with the prophecy of Jesus becoming King in Zechariah. The seventh part of the prophecy of Daniel 2 presents the installation of Christ as King. This is the Christ event to be proclaimed to the world. Jesus, now our High Priest in heaven, is to be installed as the King of kings. Before Jesus can come as King, he must *become* King.

This event in heaven will be accompanied by a great movement here on earth. The proclamation of the eternal gospel to "all people, nations and languages" that all "should serve Him" (7:14) is mirrored in the imagery of the stone becoming a great mountain and filling the earth. The paradigm shift of Jesus's ministration as High Priest to rulership as King—the inauguration and exaltation of the Son of man to the throne in Daniel 7—is affirmed and validated by the parallel prophecy of Daniel 2. The King is becoming!

"BLESSED BE THE NAME OF GOD FOREVER AND EVER:
FOR WISDOM AND MIGHT ARE HIS:
HE CHANGETH THE TIMES AND THE SEASONS:
HE REMOVETH KINGS AND SETTETH UP KINGS;
HE GIVETH WISDOM UNTO THE WISE, AND
KNOWLEDGE TO THOSE WHO HAVE
UNDERSTANDING:
HE REVEALETH DEEP AND SECRET THINGS:
HE KNOWETH WHAT IS IN THE DARKNESS, AND
LIGHT DWELLETH WITH HIM.

I THANK THEE AND PRAISE THEE, O GOD
OF MY FATHERS,
WHO HAST GIVEN ME WISDOM AND MIGHT,
AND HAST MADE KNOWN UNTO ME
NOW WHAT WE DESIRE OF THEE:
FOR THOU HAST MADE KNOWN TO US"

THE VISIONS OF THE KING
DANIEL 2:20–23

Chapter 6
Prophesy About Kings

The knowledge that right now, Jesus Christ is our Great High Priest in heaven, combined with the truth that He is coming as King of kings, leads to the logical conclusion that before He can come as King, He must *become* King. The prophecy of Zechariah 6 gave us clear and powerful evidence that just such an event—the High Priest in the midst of the Day of Atonement liturgy being placed on the throne and crowned King—has been foretold. This amazing prophecy even identifies the name of this Priest-King as Joshua, the Hebrew equivalent of Jesus.

This exciting revelation encouraged us to dig deeper into the Scriptures to search for more light on the topic of Jesus Christ becoming King. We chose a line of reasoning that followed the path of the faithful who have gone before us to examine the question of this cosmic event. We would stand on the shoulders of the founders to see if we could get a glimpse of the heavenly Canaan. We started where Miller started, with the prophecies of Daniel, to see if this event of Jesus becoming King is indeed one of the links in the chain of prophetic time.

Our search for evidence of the next Christ event in the prophecies of Daniel yielded precious and rich rewards. The Christ event that brings to completion the controversy of the Creator with His creatures over who is great and His work of redemption for and in humanity is described as giving the Son of man "dominion, and glory and a kingdom" (Dan. 7:14). The seventh part of Daniel 7 is the kingship of the Son of man.

This truth is affirmed in the parallel prophecy of Daniel 2, where the stone of judgement becomes a mountain of kingship and fills the whole earth. There can be no coincidence that these prophecies are in complete harmony with the vision of the Branch in Zechariah and supported by the testimonies of Jeremiah and Isaiah. The evidence is convincing that indeed, the next Christ event is our great High Priest is to become King!

The next step of our journey in the path of our founders is to go over the prophetic messages given to John in Revelation 10 and 14. These prophecies were the mainstay of the Millerite message and early Advent band. The hour of God's judgment was the heart of Miller's message.

The bittersweet prophecy of John explained the disappointing delay the Millerites experienced, giving the Advent band the assurance of God's blessing to remain faithful through the testing time. We are not rehashing established truths of how the prophecies were fulfilled in the Advent movement of the past. Our purpose is to reexamine the context of the prophecies for any clues that would give insight into the next event expected to occur after this prophecy was fulfilled.

Revelation 10 closes with the angel giving a command that was to carry God's messenger forward beyond the bitter disappointment and fulfill the Lord's purpose. The Advent band was commanded to "prophesy again." We briefly mentioned earlier how this charge has been the calling of the Seventh-day Adventist Church ever since. As the inheritors of the legacy, we have accepted the charge to "prophesy again about many peoples, nations, languages and kings" (v. 11, NKJV).

We recognize in this charge the familiar three-part phrase, "Peoples, nations and languages," the same phrase in Daniel 7. It was used to describe the whole kingdom or world. An excellent example is found in Daniel 4, where Nebuchadnezzar wrote his story to "all people, nations, and languages, that dwell in all the earth" (v. 1). The phrase "all the earth" helps identify the meaning of "people, nations and languages." This common, ancient, kingdom language is also found in Daniel 3, when Nebuchadnezzar issued another decree across his kingdom after the fiery furnace incident. "Therefore I make a decree, That every people, nation, and language, which speak any thing amiss against the God of Shadrach, Meshach, and Abednego, shall be cut in pieces" (v. 29, KJV).

It is not just a Babylonian thing. Darius the Mede used the same three-part phrase when writing his decree after the lions' den episode with Daniel. "Then king Darius wrote unto all people, nations, and languages, that dwell in all the earth" (6:25). Again, "all the earth" sums up what the three-part phrase "people, nations, and languages" is signifying.

This background makes the phrase "peoples, nations, languages and kings" (Rev. 10:11, NIV) stand out as odd. Why does the angel in this verse add the phrase "and kings" to the end of the otherwise common, three-part kingdom phrase, "people, nations and languages"? This gets even more intriguing when we recognize the historical context of the Millerites and the Great Disappointment of 1844. Kings and kingdoms were being erased from history.

After the French Revolution in 1798, Napoleon marched across Europe, destroying the monarchies and replacing them with republics. The French Revolution was the birth of the modern age, shaping modern culture and mindsets. Since then, kings and kingdoms have become things of fairytales and medieval history. Could it be possible that Satan was purposely trying to erase a knowledge of kings and kingdoms so that the Scriptures would become obscure, not understood by the modern mind? Since the devil doesn't want people to understand the prophecies and be prepared for the coming King, it makes sense that he would do everything possible to suppress a knowledge of these things.

> *Since then, kings and kingdoms have become things of fairytales and medieval history. Could it be possible that Satan was purposely trying to erase a knowledge of kings and kingdoms so that the Scriptures would become obscure, not understood by the modern mind?*

However, the role of the Elijah messenger is to prepare the way for the coming King (see Mark 1:2, 3; 1 Kings 18:46). Therefore, it also makes sense that God would make clear the meaning of the prophecies by instructing the Elijah messenger to prophesy again about kings. Then "knowledge shall increase" (Dan. 12:4), and people could prepare themselves for the climactic event. The fact that the phrase "and kings" is added to the common kingdom phrase of "people, nations, and languages" would stand out to anyone who was studying kings and kingdom language, like we are doing.

Since there is no other place in all of Scripture where this three-part phrase has the added "and kings," this gives added significance to the occurrence. This anomaly is peculiar to Revelation 10:11, which means it is purposeful. The call to "prophesy again about ... kings" is a clear commission to God's Elijah messenger.

In the midst of the prophecy of Revelation 10, describing John's sweet-then-bitter experience of eating the scroll, is a reference to a future event. "In the days when the seventh angel is to blow his trumpet, the mystery of God will be fulfilled, as he announced to his servants the prophets" (v. 7, NRSV). What is "the mystery of God," and what does it mean that it "should be finished" (KJV)?

Paul referred to the mystery of God: "And without controversy great is the mystery of godliness: God was manifested in the flesh, justified in the Spirit, seen of angels, preached among the Gentiles, believed on in the world, received up into glory" (1 Tim. 3:16). He described the process of God becoming a man, and the downward steps to which Jesus would submit, and then the upward process to complete our salvation. The passage reminds one of Jacob's dream and the ladder that reaches all the way down to fallen humanity and all the way back up to the throne of God, on which angels descend and ascend. The mystery of God is the unfolding of His revelation in His Son Jesus for the invitation to restoration of all that has been infected by sin.

We recognized earlier in this discussion that the mystery of iniquity that began in heaven was a decision in the mind of Lucifer "to indulge the desire for self-exaltation."[44] This "desire for supremacy" naturally set him at odds with the One in authority and His divine law that governed reality. Satan's "envy of Christ"[45] grew until it became necessary for God to clearly set forth before the hosts of heaven the authority of His Son.[46]

The conflict in heaven between Lucifer and Christ was over kingship. Because of the mystery of iniquity, Jesus came down from the throne and plunged to the depths to redeem fallen, sinful mankind. After His resurrection, He begins the process of going up, up, up. The finishing of "the

---

[44]Ellen White, Patriarchs and Prophets (Washington, DC: Review and Herald Publishing Association, 1890), p. 35.
[45]Ibid.
[46]See Ellen White, The Story of Redemption (Washington, DC: Review and Herald Publishing Association, 1947), p. 13.

mystery of God" (Rev. 10:7) is the same as the "restoration of all things" (Acts 3:21, NKJV), when Jesus is reinstated on the throne.

This testimony is in harmony with Paul's explanation of the mystery of God:

> In Him we have redemption through His blood, the forgiveness of sins, according to the riches of His grace which He made to abound toward us in all wisdom and prudence, having made known to us the mystery of His will, according to His good pleasure which He purposed in Himself, that in the dispensation of the fullness of the times He might gather together in one all things in Christ, both which are in heaven and which are on earth—in Him. (Ephesians 1:7–10, NKJV)

The finishing of the mystery is the "gather[ing] together in one all things in Christ." The exaltation of the Son back upon the throne from which he descended, to glorify His Father and save the fallen race, is the same finishing of the mystery referred to in Revelation 10:7. The finishing of the mystery is the same thing as the restoration of all things in Acts 3:19–21. These two texts parallel each other and are describing the same event. We have already established biblical evidence to support our position that Acts 3:19–21 is describing the coronation of Christ in heaven. Therefore, Revelation 10:7 must also be describing the event of Christ becoming King.

The prophecy of Revelation 10 is part of the sixth trumpet (ref. 9:13). If our understanding of the language to "prophesy again about ... kings" and the "mystery of God to be finished" in the sixth trumpet are correct about pointing to Christ becoming King, then this should become evident "in the days when the seventh angel is to blow his trumpet" (10:7, NRSV). What event occurs in the days of the seventh trumpet?

> Then the seventh angel blew his trumpet, and there were loud voices in heaven, saying, "The kingdom of the world has become the kingdom of our Lord and of his Messiah, and he will reign forever and ever." Then the twenty-four elders who sit on their thrones before God fell on their faces and worshiped God, singing, "We give you thanks, Lord God Almighty, who are and who were, for you have taken your great power and begun to reign. The nations raged, but your wrath has come, and the time for judging the dead, for rewarding your servants, the prophets and

saints and all who fear your name, both small and great, and for destroying those who destroy the earth." (Revelation 11:15–18, NRSV)

The seventh trumpet is the proclamation, "you have taken your great power and begun to reign." This language clearly describes the transition of One to the throne. The event of the seventh trumpet is beyond question. "The kingdom of the world has become the kingdom of our Lord, and of His Christ; and He will reign forever and ever" (v. 15, NASB). This event is future, not history. The Spirit of Prophecy refers to this verse as such: "The kingdoms of this world have not yet become the kingdoms of our Lord and of His Christ. Do not deceive yourselves; be wide awake and move rapidly, for the night cometh in which no man can work."[47]

"About His coming cluster the glories of that 'restitution of all things, which God hath spoken by the mouth of all His holy prophets since the world began' (Act 3:21). Then the long-continued rule of evil shall be broken; 'the kingdoms of this world' will become 'the kingdoms of our Lord, and of His Christ; and He shall reign for ever and ever' (Rev 11:15)".[48] In this quote from Sister White, we notice that she connected "the restoration of all things" in Acts 3:21 with the seventh trumpet of Revelation 11:15, which describes Christ becoming King and beginning to reign.

The direct statements of Scripture and the supporting statements of Mrs. White cannot be construed to mean anything other than the wonderful news that the seventh trumpet is the event where Christ has become King. This is the event directly referred to in Revelation 10:7: "In the days when the seventh angel is to blow his trumpet, the mystery of God will be fulfilled, as he announced to his servants the prophets" (NRSV). This is the event the angel commands us to "prophesy again about ... kings." Jesus Christ, God manifested in the flesh, who "laid aside His crown and royal robe, and stepped down from the throne, to cloth his divinity with humanity,"[49] has come full circle to be enthroned before the universe and take His rightful place as King. The mystery of God is finished. The King is becoming!

---

[47] Ellen G. White, Counsels to Parents, Teachers, and Students (Mountain View, CA: Pacific Press Publishing Association, 1913), p. 414.
[48] Ellen G. White, The Great Controversy (Mountain View, CA: Pacific Press Publishing Association, 1911), p. 301.
[49] Ellen G. White, The Desire of Ages (Mountain View, CA: Pacific Press Publishing Association, 1898), p. 410.

Chapter 7

Seated on a Cloud

We are following in the path of our founders and reexamining the prophecies that sparked the Advent movement to life because some among us believe that we are to become a present-truth movement again—a movement on earth because Christ is moving in heaven. The evidence is mounting that Jesus is about to become King, and Seventh-day Adventism is being called to "prophesy again about ... kings" (Rev. 10:11, NIV): the true King *and* the kings of the earth that oppose Him. We have looked into the prophecies of Daniel 2 and 7 because they accurately identify the flow of human history from the time of Babylon down to the second coming. We have affirmed the past truths as proclaimed by Miller and early Adventism; not a pin has been moved. Yet, standing on the shoulders of these giants, we are seeing a present-truth message for our time in the next great Christ event that is about to burst on our world.

Daniel 7 informed us that after "the court was seated, And the books were opened" (v. 9, NKJV) and the judgment commenced in heaven in 1844, the next event would be the Son of man being given "dominion, and glory, and a kingdom" (v. 14). The parallel prophecy of Daniel 2 told us that after the divine nature of the stone made manifest the humanism of the image, the stone "became a great mountain, and filled the whole earth" (v. 35). These prophecies of the next Christ event are affirmed by the angel: "In the days of the of the sounding of the seventh angel, when he is about to sound, the mystery of God would be finished" (Rev. 10:7, NKJV).

We looked at the message of the seventh angel in the seventh trumpet and discovered a clear message that coincided with what we found in the prophecies of Daniel: "The kingdoms of this world have become *the kingdoms* of our Lord and of His Christ, and He shall reign forever and ever!" (Rev. 11:15, NKJV). All are praising King Jesus because "you have taken your great power and begun to reign" (v. 17, NRSV). All the evidence points to the same glorious event. Jesus Christ is becoming King.

The three angels' messages of Revelation 14 were also foundational to the early Advent movement in warning the world and preparing themselves for the second coming of Jesus. William Miller saw in this passage messages that must be proclaimed to prepare the world for Christ's return. This rich heritage has been passed down to us. Any proclamation of the final Christ event must pass the test of being supported by and evidenced within the context of the three angels' messages.

> Deep and solemn conviction rested upon the minds of those who heard [William Miller], and ministers and people, sinners and infidels, turned to the Lord and sought a preparation to stand in the judgment. ...
>
> [Miller] ceased not to preach the everlasting gospel to crowds wherever he was invited, sounding far and near the cry, "Fear God, and give glory to Him; for the hour of His judgment is come."[50]

This precedent, established by our pioneers, beckons us to look again at the prophecy of Revelation 14:6–13. Mrs. White spoke frankly about the proclamation of the three angels. She says:[51]

> The first and second messages were given in 1843 and 1844, and we are now under the proclamation of the third; but all three of

---

[50]Ellen G. White, Early Writings (Washington, DC: Review and Herald Publishing Association, 1882), pp. 231, 232.
[51]See Ellen G. White, Selected Messages, book 2 (Washington, DC: Review and Herald Publishing Association, 1958), pp. 104, 105.

the messages are still to be proclaimed. It is just as essential now as ever before that they shall be repeated to those who are seeking for the truth. By pen and voice we are to sound the proclamation, showing their order, and the application of the prophecies that bring us to the third angel's message. There cannot be a third without the first and the second. These messages we are to give to the world in publications, in discourses, showing in the line of prophetic history the things that have been, and the things that will be.

This amazing quote nails down the historicity of three angels' message in the Millerite movement, as well as foretells the reviving of these messages at some point in the future. Looking at Revelation 14:6–13 from this historical perspective, it should be easy for us to determine the next significant event from the content of the verses that follow. What do verses 14–20 describe as the next significant event? "Then I looked, and behold, a white cloud, and on the cloud sat One like the Son of Man, having on His head a golden crown, and in His hand a sharp sickle" (v. 14, NKJV).

The Son of man sits on a cloud having a crown of gold upon his head. This word picture is a combination of the symbols and biblical imagery in Daniel 7:13 (Son of man with the clouds of heaven) and Zechariah 6:11 (golden crown upon His head). We looked already at cloud symbolism and the myriads of angels that make up His throne chariot. This symbolism is unmistakable. Revelation 14 places the future proclamation of the three angels' messages in the context of Jesus becoming King in heaven.

Consistent with Zechariah, Jeremiah, and Isaiah, there is a gathering, a great harvest, that is connected to the kingship of Christ (see Rev. 14:14–20). The King has a "sharp sickle in his hand" (v. 14, NIV). He orchestrates the movements on earth that constitute the harvest. This confirms what we have consistently discovered at every point: the kingship of Jesus is the next event, in the context of which the harvest of the earth takes place.

The recent evidence made available in the seventh part of Daniel 7 confirms the connection of the Son of man's installation as King in heaven with the first angels' message of Revelation 14. The content of the seven parts of Daniel 7 precisely mirrors the content of the first angels' message of Revelation 14:6–7.

Daniel 7:13–14	Revelation 14:6–7
"His dominion is everlasting"	"everlasting gospel"
"all the peoples, nations and languages"	"every nation language tribe and people"
"To him was given dominion and glory"	"fear God and give him glory"
"Kingship" (The King is Judge, Isa. 33:22)	"the hour of his judgment"
"all the peoples … should serve Him"	"worship him that Created"

Christ's dominion and kingship are described in harmony with His divine, everlasting nature. This everlasting dominion, so "that all people, nations, and languages, should serve him" (Dan. 7:14), is the everlasting gospel that will go forth in its fullness (see Rev. 14:6). The three stages of the proclamation of the King in Daniel 7:13–14 to all the people, nations, and languages is the same eternal gospel given by the three angels' messages in Revelation 14:6–12. Since the King is the Creator (see Isa. 43:15), the call to worship the Creator is a call to serve the King and partake in His everlasting kingdom. This proclamation will be the fullness of which 1844 was a forerunner. Remember Mrs. White's statement: "The power which stirred the people so mightily in the 1844 movement will again be revealed."[52]

In light of the truth of Christ becoming King, clearly set forth in the prophecies, and our call to "prophesy again about" the King as a present-truth message, let us review that amazing quote from Mrs. White:

> The first and second messages were given in 1843 and 1844, and we are now under the proclamation of the third; but all three of the messages are still to be proclaimed. It is just as essential now as ever before that they shall be repeated to those who are seeking for the truth. By pen and voice we are to sound the proclamation, showing their order, and the application of the prophecies that bring us to the third angel's message. There cannot be a third without the first and the second. These messages we are to give to the world in publications, in discourses, showing in the line of

---

[52]Ellen G. White, Testimonies for the Church, vol. 5 (Mountain View, CA: Pacific Press Publishing Association, 1889), p. 252.

prophetic history the things that have been, and the things that will be.[53]

- All three messages are still to be proclaimed
- It is as essential now as ever before that they shall be repeated to those who are seeking truth
- Showing their order and the application of the prophecies
- Showing in the line of prophetic history the things that have been ...
- And the things that will be

"Now" is the time "for those who are seeking truth." The kingship of Christ is the event shown in the line of prophetic history. Is there any doubt that it is "the things that will be" to which Mrs. White is referring?[54]

Revelation 14:14 presents Jesus as the King. A clear transition has occurred from His high-priestly ministry that was the revelation of truth to the Millerite remnant after 1844. This truth presents a huge paradigm shift. Up to this point in the history of the Christian church, the ministration of Jesus for the salvation of humanity has taken him into the sanctuary. Since His atoning death on the cross and resurrection, Jesus has been ascending up and into the heavenly sanctuary. From Pentecost in AD 31 to his high-priestly, day of atonement ministration in 1844, Jesus has been moving in the sanctuary.

Revelation 14:14–20 describes a huge paradigm shift. Jesus is no longer going in; now He is coming out. He went in as our Sacrifice, the Lamb that was slain, and our High Priest. He comes out as our King. This change of ministration is emphasized in the text by the change of direction.

After describing the cloud throne, John sees the Son of man seated in the place of authority with a golden crown on His head and a sharp sickle in His hand (see v. 14). He then observes "another angel came out of the temple" (v. 15). Again, "another angel came out of the temple which is in heaven" (v. 17). A third time, John observes "another angel came out from the altar" (v. 18). The message cannot be any clearer.

The movement and direction of the ministration of Jesus has transitioned from priestly to kingly; from going in to coming out. He has become King and initiates the process of coming out. This coming-out process of

---

[53]Ellen G. White, Selected Messages, book 2 (Washington, DC: Review and Herald Publishing Association, 1958), pp. 104, 105.
[54]See Ellen G. White, Ye Shall Receive Power (Hagerstown, MD: Review and Herald Publishing Association, 1995), p. 182.

the King is accompanied by a "loud voice" (v. 15) and "loud cry" (v. 18). The message of the revelation of Christ becoming King is accompanied by a "loud cry" message that ripens the harvest of the earth. Daniel described it this way: "The stone that struck the image became a great mountain and filled the whole earth" (2:35, NKJV). Additionally, "One like the Son of Man came with the clouds of heaven, and came to the Ancient of days, and they brought him near before him. And there was given him dominion and glory, and a kingdom, that all people, nations, and languages, should serve Him" (7:13, 14).

> *The proclamation of Christ becoming King is to fill the earth and go forth to all people, nations, and languages. This message is the loud cry of the third angel that is to bring the harvest of the earth, both good and evil, to maturity, in preparation for the glorious second coming of Jesus.*

The proclamation of Christ becoming King is to fill the earth and go forth to all people, nations, and languages. This message is the loud cry of the third angel that is to bring the harvest of the earth, both good and evil, to maturity, in preparation for the glorious second coming of Jesus.

We have followed the path of our founders and reexamined the prophecies that sparked the early Advent movement to life. We have affirmed the past truths as proclaimed by Miller and early Adventism; not a pin has been moved. Yet, standing on the shoulders of these giants, we are seeing a present-truth message for our time in the next great Christ event that is about to happen. The evidence is obvious, consistent, and amazing.

The prophecies of Daniel 2 and 7 establish the line of prophetic history from the time of Babylon down to our time of Christ becoming King. The prophecy of Revelation 10 gives a powerful command for Seventh-day Adventism to "prophesy again about ... kings" (v. 11, NKJV). "The days of the sounding of the seventh angel, when he is about to sound" (v. 7, NKJV) are upon us. It is time that "the mystery of God should be finished." The Son of man is about to take His great power and begin to reign (see 11:15). The loud cry of the third angel is to accompany the King of kings, bringing the harvest of the earth to maturity.

It is the conviction of this author, from the picture painted by the prophecies examined in this study, that Jesus is to become King. This is the next great Christ event that is about to rock this world. This event will ignite into flame the chain of events that will, in quick succession, bring to maturity the final events about which we have been prophesying for over 150 years.

The King is be-coming!!!

Chapter 8
According to the Custom

After the bitter disappointment of 1844, the mighty Angel of Revelation 10 commanded His servant, "thou must prophesy again about ... kings" (v. 11, NKJV). Why would the Lord instruct His remnant people to prophesy about kings? Adventism has long-recognized the historical date of 1798 as the beginning of the time of the end. We see how Satan worked at this time to remove all knowledge of kings and kingdoms. The French Revolution was the birth of the modern age, introducing the republic as an alternative form of governance. Napoleon marched across Europe, destroying monarchies to such an extent that, though they survived for a short period after his demise, their end was a foregone conclusion. The dawn of modernity was the death knell of the monarchy.

Time and distance have eroded the knowledge of the dynamics of kings and kingdoms to the point of being lost. In this context, prophesying again about kings would make available those truths that had been lost and open the eyes of modernity to the mysteries in God's Holy Word concerning the establishment of His kingdom.

The sealed book in Daniel 12 has a direct connection with the open book in Revelation 10. Daniel was told in the end that "knowledge shall be increased" (12:4). Could it be to prepare a dark, sin-sick planet for the coming of the Sun of Righteousness to rise with healing in His wings (see Mal. 4:1)?

This purposeful ignorance of kingdom and kingship dynamics is part of the reason that so many people don't know, haven't heard, and never even thought about the transition of Christ from High Priest to King. Much of what scholars do know about ancient kingship is not based on the Bible, but on other pagan cultures. It's true that this can lend insight into some of the customs and rituals common to most kingdoms, but God's kingdom established in Israel was unique; it was to be set apart for a holy purpose. We must be attentive that our understanding of God's pattern for kingship comes from His Word.

It's right that many questions arise surrounding our thesis of Jesus being installed as King in heaven before He can return. This is by far the greatest Christ event that the world will have ever experienced. The coming of the King in His glory was what the Jews expected at the first coming of Jesus Christ. That's one of the reasons they did not recognize the babe in a manger or accept the humble Galilean. In fact, every Christ event throughout the salvation process has been misunderstood and misinterpreted by God's people.

> ***This purposeful ignorance of kingdom and kingship dynamics is part of the reason that so many people don't know, haven't heard, and never even thought about the transition of Christ from High Priest to King.***

The coming of the King in glory will come "unawares" to the world (Luke 21:34), but it cannot be mistaken by God's people. There will be no "Oops, we got it wrong. Let's study it out and make a correction." Not this time. The finality of the event and the eternal consequences demand that everyone understand and choose before Jesus comes.

This is one of the special truths that we have for the world. Probation closes before Jesus comes. This gives great urgency to the three angels' messages. For probation to close, there must be great light that shines to the world concerning the King. The "wise shall shine as the brightness of the firmament; and they that turn many to righteousness as the stars for ever and ever" (Dan. 12:3). "Many shall be purified, and made white, and tried; but the wicked shall do wickedly: and none of the wicked shall understand; but the wise shall understand" (v. 10, KJV). This battle of the kings, or the time of trouble, will precede the second coming of Christ. Therefore, it is important for us to be wise concerning the dynamics of the kingship and critical of speculation. Our knowledge must be based on God's Word.

The discussion in this chapter is an attempt to establish a biblical foundation for the process of one becoming king in ancient Israel that will give insights into the Messianic fulfilment in Christ's ministry for our salvation. From this, we will attempt to answer of few of the fundamental questions directly surrounding the idea of kingship and remove some of the baggage that stands in the way of understanding its relevance to us today. One of the first questions asked is, "Hasn't Jesus always been King?" This question combines with, "Didn't Mrs. White tell us that Jesus was coronated at His crucifixion?" If Jesus is already King, then what's this becoming King before He *comes* as King?

Yes, Jesus is, was, and is to come, the King of kings. And yes, Mrs. White clearly identifies His crucifixion as His coronation. "[Jesus] prayed for his disciples. They were to be grievously tried. Their long-cherished hopes, based on a popular delusion, were to be disappointed in a most painful and humiliating manner. In the place of His exaltation to the throne of David they were to witness His crucifixion. This was to be indeed His true coronation."[55]

Indeed, the crucifixion of Christ was a true coronation. The King was anointed with oil by a prostitute (see John 12:3–8), clothed in a purple robe by an immoral ruler (see Luke 23:11), crowned with thorns by rude, hardened soldiers (see John 19:2), given a scepter of reeds while being mocked and spit upon by a careless mob (see v. 3), scourged with a whip as an acknowledgement of His authority, and rejected by His own people, who boldly exclaimed, "We have no king but Caesar" (v. 15).

A procession of humiliation and abuse guided Him to His place of honor. He was exalted to His place of authority by spikes and a wooden cross and set as a Prince among criminals. Above his head hung the proclamation, written in three languages for the entire world to read, "JESUS OF NAZARETH, THE KING OF THE JEWS" (v. 19). Even though this event occurred in public, only one person in the whole crowd understood and acknowledged Jesus as his King: the thief on the cross. "Lord, remember me when You come into Your kingdom" (Luke 23:42, NKJV). To all extents and purposes, His coronation at Calvary happened in secret.

---

[55]Ellen G. White, The Desire of Ages (Mountain View, CA: Pacific Press Pub Association, 1898), p. 379.

If so, then why would He need to be coronated again in heaven before He comes? Why are we studying the Bible to understand Christ's coronation if the event has already occurred? The question makes evident our lack of understanding of the biblical process of being installed as king. We think of the coronation of a king as a one-time event—the person to be king is coronated, and that's it, he's king. However, the Bible presents a process of installing a king that contains three stages. Each step or stage is critical, without which the whole process collapses. For a biblical understanding of the process of kingship, let's go to 1 and 2 Samuel and examine the installation of the first two kings in Israel.

After the death of Eli, "Samuel judged Israel all the days of his life" (1 Sam. 7:15), but when Samuel was old, "all the elders of Israel gathered themselves together, and came to Samuel unto Ramah, And said unto him, Behold, thou art old, and thy sons walk not in thy ways: now make us a king to judge us like all the nations" (8:4, 5, KJV). This "displeased" Samuel, but the Lord told Samuel, "Heed the voice of the people in all that they say to you; for they have not rejected you, but they have rejected Me, that I should not reign over them" (8:7, NKJV). Samuel warned the people of what would happen, but the people responded, "No, but we will have a king over us" (v. 19). Samuel followed God's direction and anointed Saul as king (see 10:1). This anointing as king was, as it were, done in secret. No one knew but Samuel and Saul.

Then Samuel "called all of Israel to the LORD at Mizpah" (v. 17) and challenged them: "present yourselves before the LORD by your tribes, and by your thousands" (v. 19). Lots were cast, and the tribe of Benjamin was chosen; then the family of Matri was chosen; then Saul the son of Kish was chosen (see vs. 20, 21). Saul was presented to Israel as God's chosen, and "all the people shouted and said, 'Long live the king!'" (v. 24). "But some rebels said, 'How can this man save us? So they despised him, and brought him no presents'" (v. 27).

Saul was presented as king but was not yet king. Not all the people acknowledged or accepted him as their king. He must first demonstrate power through victory over his enemies before he can be installed as king. Saul does this by delivering the city of Jabesh Gilead. "Then Samuel said to the people, 'Come, let us go to Gilgal[56] and renew the kingdom there.

---

[56] Gilgal was the place of installing the king because it was here where Israel camped after crossing the Jordan and Joshua was installed as the new leader of Israel after the death of Moses. It was here at Gilgal, before Jericho where Joshua encountered the "Captain of the Lord's Host" (Josh 5:14), fell on his face, and worshiped because the Lord is the King over His people.

So all the people went to Gilgal, and there they made Saul king before the LORD at Gilgal'" (11:14, 15, NKJV). Chapter 12 is the record of Saul's coronation. Samuel charges the people with misconduct and warns them against future disobedience. The Lord responds by sending "thunder and rain" (v. 18).

Saul has been installed twice and begins to reign. "Saul reigned one year; and when he had reigned two years over Israel, Saul chose for himself three thousand men of Israel" (13:1, NKJV). Israel gets into a conflict with the Philistines, "And the people were called together to Saul at Gilgal" (v. 4). Here, Saul waits for Samuel "seven days," but Samuel did not come, so Saul "offered the burnt offering" (vs. 8, 9). This sin is grievous because Saul the king is taking to himself priestly authority. Saul is not, nor can be, the priest-king. Only One who is to come can and will fulfill that place.

Political and religious authority was to remain separate and distinct in Israel until the One to whom it rightfully belonged would come. Saul is arrogant and prideful, taking authority to himself that is not his. The seriousness of this crime is made evident by Samuel's response: "You have done foolishly. You have not kept the commandment of the LORD your God, which He commanded you. For now the LORD would have established your kingdom over Israel forever. But now your kingdom shall not continue" (vs. 13, 14). To this sin, Saul adds the sin of disobedience by not following God's instructions in terms of the Amalekites. It's as if God is giving Saul another chance to vindicate himself, but Saul fails to obey His voice. "Now the word of the LORD came to Samuel, saying, 'I greatly regret that I have set up Saul as king, for he has turned back from following Me'" (15:10, 11, NKJV). Saul is not installed as king the third time. His kingship is not affirmed. He is rejected as the king, and the kingdom is torn from him and given to another (see v. 28).

Here, we see a three-stage process of the king being installed in Israel. The first time, Saul is anointed as king, but nobody knows it because he is alone. The second time, Saul is coronated as king before some of the people, but not everyone accepts him as king. However, because of Saul's unfaithfulness, he never sees the third and final coronation that would have established his kingdom and lineage forever. His kingship and kingdom are given to a boy named David.

Samuel is sent by the Lord to anoint a son of Jesse: "For I have provided me a king among his sons" (16:1, NKJV). David is chosen, and "Samuel took the horn of oil and anointed him" (v. 13). Again, no one knows but a very few. David lives in obscurity, but the Lord works all things together to result in good and brings David to the throne. After the death of Saul, David is coronated the second time. "Then the men of Judah came, and there they anointed David king over the house of Judah" (2 Sam. 2:4, NJKV).

Israel fights against David but doesn't' prevail. Then "all the elders of Israel came to the king at Hebron ... And they anointed David king over Israel" (5:3). After this third and final coronation, David is established as the king over all Israel and promised that he will perpetually have a son to rule; that His kingdom will never end. The Son of David will rule on the throne of His Father forever (see 7:13).

The three-stage process of establishing the Davidic kingdom is important and made clear by the repetition of the process that was almost completed by Saul. The first anointing as king is quiet and unnoticed, like a lonely man crucified on a dark hill or a horn of oil raised over the head of a small boy who tends the sheep. The future king is all alone, and it seems humanly impossible that he would ever fulfill the destiny of reigning on the throne. The second coronation occurs, but only some of the people acknowledge and accept the newly installed king. The third and final coronation of the king occurs when all of Israel acknowledges and accepts David as its king. His kingship is established perpetually, and so from his line the Messiah will come.

> *The three-stage process of establishing the Davidic kingdom is important and made clear by the repetition of the process that was almost completed by Saul. The first anointing as king is quiet and unnoticed, like a lonely man crucified on a dark hill or a horn of oil raised over the head of a small boy who tends the sheep.*

This biblical pattern and historical process becomes a prophecy of the process of establishing the Lion of the tribe of Judah, the root and offspring of David, who will reign forever.

Christ was also coronated the first time all alone; the act was completed with the cry, "It is finished" (John 19:30). It seemed humanly impossible that this Man from Nazareth would ever gain the throne, but death could not hold the Lord of glory, and He has ascended to the heavenly sanctuary to mediate for lost humanity until the time comes for His second installation: the transition from His priestly ministration to His kingship.

According to the prophetic pattern, the second coronation of the king will be acknowledged by those who are His, but not all. The second coronation of Christ is what we are studying and attempting to understand. It is the present truth of our time. The second coronation will also be followed with the declaration from the throne, "It is done!" (Rev. 16:17).

> We are homeward bound. He who loved us so much as to die for us hath builded for us a city. The New Jerusalem is our place of rest. There will be no sadness in the City of God. No wail of sorrow, no dirge of crushed hopes and buried affections, will evermore be heard. Soon the garments of heaviness will be changed for the wedding garment. Soon we shall witness the coronation of our King. Those whose lives have been hidden with Christ, those who on this earth have fought the good fight of faith, will shine forth with Redeemer's glory in the kingdom of God.[57]

The third and final coronation of the King, according to the prophetic model, will be acknowledged by all. "That at the name of Jesus every knee should bow, of things in heaven, and things in earth, and things under the earth; And that every tongue should confess that Jesus Christ is Lord, to the glory of God the Father" (Phil. 2:10, 11). Mrs. White described this event. After the thousand years, the New Jerusalem comes down from heaven, and the resurrected wicked surround the golden city.

> Now Christ again appears to the view of His enemies. Far above the city, upon a foundation of burnished gold, is a throne, high and lifted up. Upon this throne sits the Son of God, and around Him are the subjects of His kingdom. The power and majesty of Christ no language can describe, no pen portray. The glory of the Eternal Father is enshrouding His Son. ...
>
> In the presence of the assembled inhabitants of earth and heaven the final coronation of the Son of God takes place. And now, invested with supreme majesty and power, the King of kings pronounces sentence upon the rebels against His government and executes justice upon those who have transgressed His law and oppressed His people. ...

---

[57]Ellen G. White, The Adventist Home (Hagerstown, MD: Review and Herald Publishing Association, 1952), pp. 542, 543.

> As if entranced, the wicked have looked upon the coronation of the Son of God. ...
>
> [Satan] has seen the crown placed upon the head of Christ by an angel of lofty stature and majestic presence, and he knows that the exalted position of this angel might have been his.[58]

The plan of salvation is complete. No more sin; no more sorrow; no more night. At Christ's third and final coronation, He declares, for the third and final time, the same phrase that accompanied the first two coronations: "It is done" (Rev. 21:6).

In Christ, we see the typical pattern of David becoming king fulfilled. His first coronation is, as it were, in secret, alone, and seemingly impossible to ever happen, but "it is done." The second coronation is understood and accepted by some, but not all will receive their king. Still, it is done. The third and final coronation of Christ will be seen and acknowledged by every living creature. Then the King of Righteousness will declare that the reign of sin and rebellion against His government will be ended. It is done!

This is the biblical, three-stage pattern of the installation of the King in the kingdom of God.

---

[58] Ellen G. White, The Great Controversy (Mountain View, CA: Pacific Press Publishing Association, 1911), pp. 665–669.

Just a Thought #1

Jesus was anointed by the Holy Spirit at each stage of His ministration. This inaugural anointing took on some form of physical display that was visible and tangible to those around Him. He was anointed at his baptism. John saw the Holy Spirit in the form of a dove and heard a voice from heaven (see Matt. 3:16). Jesus went forth proclaiming, "[God] hath anointed me to preach the gospel to the poor" (Luke 4:18, NKJV). At the end of His ministry, Mary anoints Him for His burial, and the whole house is filled with the fragrance of the oil (see John 12:3, 7). This event is so significant that two Gospels stated, "wherever this gospel is preached in the whole world, what this woman has done will also be told as a memorial to her" (Matt. 26:13; Mark 14:9, NKJV).

After His resurrection, Jesus ascended to heaven, and there, He was anointed for His priestly ministry on the day of Pentecost. Peter bears witness: "[Jesus] has received from the Father the promised Holy Spirit and has poured out what you now see and hear" (Acts 2:33, NIV). Jesus has been ministering in the heavenly sanctuary as our High Priest from then until today (see Heb. 8:1, 2). Since He was anointed by God at every transitional stage of His ministry to prepare and empower Him for the next phase of His work of salvation, why would we think it strange or unnecessary for Him to be anointed and installed as King before He becomes King?

Our confusion is par for the course. At every transitional stage of Christ's ministry, when He was anointed for His next phase, God's people did not know or understand what was happening. Their expectation was consistently out of touch with the reality of the situation. "The light shines in the darkness, and the darkness did not comprehend it" (John 1:5, NKJV).

Not only did they not understand, but as Stephen accurately testified, "You always resist the Holy Spirit; as your fathers did, so do you" (Acts 7:51, NKJV). Opposition was consistently voiced during each of the anointing inauguration events. John questioned the necessity of baptizing Jesus and resisted the ceremony, just as the last-day Elijah questions the need for Jesus to be anointed as King. However, Jesus said to him, "Permit it to be so now, for thus it is fitting for us to fulfill all righteousness" (Matt. 3:15, NKJV). Again, when Mary anointed Christ's body for burial, the disciples questioned the necessity of the ceremony and grumbled about the cost. When Jesus was anointed in heaven as Priest at Pentecost, and the benefits overflowed to His disciples, in ignorance the people mocked and accused the disciples of being "full of new wine" (Acts 2:13).

God's people have consistently misunderstood and misinterpreted every event of Christ's salvation ministry. From His birth in the manger to His death on the cross, the Spirit of truth had to warn against missing the event or explain its meaning. Even when the prophecies clearly define the timing of the event, from His crucifixion to 1844, we have misinterpreted, misunderstood, and had to have it explained to us after the fact. That's why Jesus repeatedly warned us about His coming. The Son of man is coming at an hour you do not expect (see Matt. 24:44, 50; 25:13; Luke 12:40).

However, there is huge difference between the second coming and the other Christ events. In the past, we misunderstood the event but had time and opportunity to correct our mistake. Concerning the second coming, there will be no "Oops, we misunderstood" or an opportunity to make an adjustment. The finality of the event must be explained, understood, and decided before the event occurs. This truth makes the inauguration of Christ as King and the resulting proclamation of the three angels' messages all the more significant. Our consistent track record of misunderstanding and misinterpreting the event should give us a spirit of humility and cautious, prayerful concern. The wise people of this world never accepted the truth of the event, even after it was explained to them. Their pride would not allow them to accept the fact that they were wrong and God passed by the wise and learned to give insight to the lowly and poor.

Jesus has been anointed at every transitional stage of His ministry. Why wouldn't He be anointed for His kingship as He transitions from Priest to King? It only makes sense that He will be anointed again as King before He *comes* as King. At every previous stage, we have misunderstood the event. Are we still so sure of ourselves that we are not even going to investigate the Scriptures to see if these things are true?

Chapter 9

The Faithful and True Witness

"And this gospel of the kingdom shall be preached in all the world for a witness unto all nations; and then the end will come" (Matt. 24:14). Jesus states that the "gospel of the kingdom" has a direct bearing on "the end," identifying a concrete cause-and-effect relationship between the two. Both concepts are specified as facts: the gospel of the kingdom "shall be" preached, then the end "shall" come. Our discussion of the kingship of Christ is an attempt to highlight the importance of the kingdom part of the Lord's declaration.

How can the gospel of the kingdom be fully proclaimed when there is no king? You cannot have a kingdom without a king. This was the intent of the apostles' question after His resurrection. "Lord, will you at this time restore the kingdom to Israel?" (Acts 1:6, NKJV). The Lord's response is insightful: "He said to them, 'It is not for you to know times or seasons which the Father has put in His own authority'" (v. 7, NKJV). What does Jesus mean by "times and seasons?"

The same phrase is found in Daniel 2. Daniel is praising God in response to the insights given to him about Nebuchadnezzar's dream of the image, saying, "[God] changes the times and the seasons; He removes kings and raises up kings" (v. 21, NKJV). The phrase "times and seasons" describes the setting up and deposing of kings and kingdoms. Jesus recognizes the disciples' question about "restoring the kingdom" to mean His exaltation to the throne by the Father. He acknowledges to His disciples that there can be no restoration of the kingdom without the restoration of the King. He also acknowledges that it will happen sometime in the future, but it's not for them to know the "times and seasons."

The proclamation of the gospel of the kingdom will fully go forth when the King has taken His rightful place, then the end will come. This is the conclusion from all the biblical evidence we have seen so far. The inauguration of Christ in heaven as King is the event that initiates all last-day events and the present-truth message for us to whom the ends of the earth have come.

To speak of the end is to speak of the church of Laodicea. Laodicea is the end-time church. If the restoration of Jesus to the throne is the last event in His ministry for the salvation of humanity, then the end-time church must have a knowledge of these things to be able to proclaim them. It is only logical to conclude, then, that Jesus would deliberately refer to His role as King in His message to Laodicea, just in case, for some strange reason, Laodicea might become distracted by the wisdom of the world and lose track of what is most important. There is something about Jesus standing outside, knocking to gain entrance, and calling, "if any man hear my voice" (Rev. 3:20) to a people who are asleep because they think they are "rich, and increased with goods, and have need of nothing" (v. 17).

It is a reasonable hypothesis, then, that if the kingship of Jesus is a critical component of the gospel of the kingdom that goes to the whole world before the end comes, it will be readily apparent in His message to Laodicea. This is another way to test the credibility of our conclusions. If the kingship of Christ is prevalent in the message to Laodicea, then not only does it verify this as the event that brings the end, but it may also be the very revelation of truth for Laodicea to cure her sickness, awaken her from her lukewarm state, and overcome her friendship with the world.

Let's examine the straight testimony of the True Witness to the church of Laodicea and see if Christ's kingship has anything to do with the message. As in all our previous studies of the Scriptures, it is not intended to be an exhaustive study of the message to the church of Laodicea. We are looking to verify the biblical accuracy of the thesis that before Jesus can come as King, He must *become* King. Before we jump into the text, some brief background about Laodicea is in order.

Laodicea is an Adventist swear word—a phrase accepted as applying to the church as a whole, but seldom applied individually or personally to oneself. It conveniently describes others, but not me! There are two types of people in the church of Laodicea: those who acknowledge that they are Laodicean, "wretched, and miserable, and poor, and blind, and naked" (Rev. 3:17), and those who don't believe they are. Of course, thinking that you are not is the very definition of the Laodicean condition. Welcome to Laodicea! Being lukewarm means being "'rich; I have acquired wealth and do not need a thing.' But you do not realize that you are wretched, pitiful, poor, blind and naked" (NIV).

> *Laodicea is an Adventist swear word—a phrase accepted as applying to the church as a whole, but seldom applied individually or personally to oneself. It conveniently describes others, but not me!*

Adventists have traditionally seen the label of "Laodicean" in a derogatory sense, but that's part of our blindness. We think we are better than that, which is undeniable evidence that we are "wretched, miserable, poor, blind and naked"—Laodicean. We have been slow to accept the total depravity of our fallen nature: "the heart is deceitful above all things and desperately wicked" (Jer. 17:9); "There is none righteous, no, not one" (Rom. 3:10). Not seeing our total helplessness makes us oblivious to the reality of our desperate need for "THE LORD OUR RIGHTEOUSNESS" (Jer. 23:6). As the saying goes, "Only sick people need a doctor."

"Laodicea" is not a negative term. The word literally means "people of judgment"; it can also be translated "right people." The description can be positive or negative based on the individual's acknowledgment or denial of one's condition. Traditionally, Laodicea has viewed itself as "right" because it has the truth. All our "right" information and correct doctrinal positions have given rise to spiritual arrogance, as if we are a group of righteous people just waiting for Jesus to hurry up and take us to heaven. This attitude of superiority has grieved away the Spirit of Christ, and we are left in a lukewarm state. However, if we can hear the voice of the One who stands at the door and knocks and let Him in, we could become "right people."

Nevertheless, how can we choose if we are not aware of our condition and the available options from which to choose. Like Saul of Tarsus, zealously serving God, we, Laodicea, need a revelation of Christ to knock us off our high horse and open our eyes to our spiritual blindness. Could the revelation of Jesus as King be the light that exposes our blindness? Like Saul, Laodicea needs a revelation of her Lord that will bring her to realize her true condition and acknowledge her great need. This discussion has everything to do with the kingship of Christ because He is THE LORD OUR RIGHTEOUSNESS.

Again, Laodicea means "people of judgment." According to Scripture, judgment is a kingly function. "For the LORD is our judge, the LORD is our lawgiver, the LORD is our king; he will save us" (Isa. 33:22). "Give the king thy judgments, O God, and thy righteousness to the king's son. He shall judge thy people with righteousness, and the poor with judgment" (Ps. 72:1, 2). The King is the judge because He is the source and standard of righteousness.

Laodicea is living in the "hour of His judgment" (Rev. 14:6, NKJV). This judgment process actually begins with them, since "judgment must begin at the house of God" (1 Peter 4:17). Then it makes sense that God's church at this time would be called Laodicean, "people of judgment." Laodicea lives at the time when the King is to weigh the characters and examine His subjects. The very name "Laodicea," "people of judgment," screams kingship.

"To the angel of the Church of the Laodiceans write: 'These are the words of the Amen, the faithful and true witness, the ruler of God's creation.'" (Rev. 3:14, NIV). In each of the messages to the seven churches, the description of Christ fits the nature and experience of the respective church. His characteristics are the remedy for what ails His struggling people. The description of Christ at the introduction to each of the churches identifies the traits of character to be adopted by and reflected in those who are to be overcomers. For Laodicea, this means that the three-part description of Christ via His titles at the beginning of His straight testimony is the medicine for the church's illness. Jesus presents Himself to His "people of judgment" as "the Amen, the faithful and true witness, the ruler of God's creation."

The title "Amen" is profound in a variety of applications. When the ancients wanted to describe what is true—reality as a whole—they used the term "amen." The basic meaning of "amen" is "what is certain or what is true."[59] The term "amen" is the summation of all reality. Let's examine biblical insight into the concept of "amen" that helps explain the context of its use in John's Apocalypse:

> And every creature which is in heaven and on the earth and under the earth and such as are in the sea, and all that are in them, I heard saying: "Blessing and honor and glory and power *Be* to Him who sits on the throne, And to the Lamb, forever and ever!" Then the four living creatures said, "Amen!" And the twenty-four elders fell down and worshiped Him who lives forever and ever. (Revelation 5:13, 14, NKJV)

The context of this passage is all-inclusive. It starts out with "every creature" and then goes on to identify every possible realm: "in heaven, on the earth and under the earth and such as are in the sea." It ends by restating the total inclusivity intended by the phrase "all that are in them"—all creatures in every domain, including every race and class, without distinction.

What are "all" doing? All are saying, "Blessing and honor and glory and power be to Him who sits on the throne, and to the Lamb" (v. 13). Yes, they are praising and worshipping "Him who sits on the throne, and the Lamb"—the King. Earlier in the chapter, the Lamb is "standing at the center of the throne" (v. 6, NIV). The Son has actually joined His Father on the throne to co-reign with Him. The King is both the Father and the Son.

The last inclusive element is time, "forever and ever" (v. 13), which means eternity. In the context of all creatures, in all space and time, giving glory to the One who sits on the throne, the four living creatures say, "Amen" (v. 14). This demonstrates how the term "amen" is employed in Revelation to describe the summation of all reality in reference to Jesus in His kingly role.

Psalm 72 is a royal psalm describing the kingly honors conferred on the Son by the Father. "Give the king thy judgments, O God, and thy righteousness to the king's son" (v. 1). The psalm goes on to explain the extent of His reign and authority. In terms of space, "He will rule from sea to sea and from the River to the ends of the earth" (v. 8, NIV); in terms of time, "as long as the sun, and as long as the moon, through all generations"

---

[59]Laird Harris, Theological Wordbook of the Old Testament (Chicago: Moody Press, 1980), p. 51.

(v. 5, NIV); in terms of people, "all kings bow down to him and all nations serve him" (v. 11, NIV).

The beautiful language of the psalm proceeds to describe the glory and majesty of the compassionate king who "will deliver the needy" (v. 12) and rescues the afflicted. He brings riches of abundance and peace. The eloquence of the psalm is summed up in these words: "Blessed be the LORD God, the God of Israel, Who only does wondrous things! And blessed be His glorious name forever! And let the whole earth be filled with His glory. Amen and Amen" (v. 19, NKJV). Again, the concept of "amen" is applied to the summation of all reality—space, time, creation, and humanity in reference to the Son of God in His kingly role.

Isaiah, describing the restoration from sin and the end of the "former troubles" (65:16), introduced God with a new name: "Because he who is blessed in the earth Will be blessed by the God of [Amen];[60] And he who swears in the earth Will swear by the God of [Amen]" (NASB). The Hebrew word, translated as "truth" in the KJV, NKJV, ASV, and NASB, is *aw-mane'*, literally "amen." Amen is God's new name. Then he said, "For behold, I create new heavens and a new earth" (v. 17). "Amen" is "another name" (v. 15) of the God of creation who makes all things new.

According to the Scriptures, the act of creation is a kingly function: "I am the LORD, your Holy One, the creator of Israel, your King" (43:15). We see biblical authors employ the concept of "amen" to describe the creatures' description of and response to the King of creation, who encompasses all reality. This truth is repeated in the third title of Christ given to Laodicea; we will look at that in a moment: "the [Gr. *arche'*] of creation." The point being made here is that the title of "The Amen" to Laodicea, as interpreted and defined by Scripture, is a description of Jesus Christ in His kingly ministration of creation, or a new creation (see 2 Cor. 5:17), the eternal gospel.

The second description of Jesus to Laodicea is "the faithful and true witness." Again, the use of the title in another place in Revelation demonstrates the contextual application and gives insight to discern its meaning. "Faithful and True" is also the designation of the Rider on the white horse:

> Now I saw heaven opened, and behold, a white horse. And He who sat on him *was* called Faithful and True, and in righteousness He judges and makes war. His eyes *were* like a flame of fire, and

---

[60] Hebrew *aw-mane'*, translated "truth" (NASB), is literally "Amen."

on His head *were* many crowns. He had a name written that no one knew except Himself. He *was* clothed with a robe dipped in blood, and His name is called The Word of God. And the armies in heaven, clothed in fine linen, white and clean, followed Him on white horses. Now out of His mouth goes a sharp sword, that with it He should strike the nations. And He Himself will rule them with a rod of iron. He Himself treads the winepress of the fierceness and wrath of Almighty God. And He has on *His* robe and on His thigh a name written: KING OF KINGS AND LORD OF LORDS. (Revelation 19:11–16, NKJV)

He who is called "Faithful and True" judges in righteousness. "On His head are many crowns." "He will rule all nations with a rod of iron." He is "KING OF KINGS AND LORD OF LORDS." There is no question that the title "Faithful and True" is a reference to Christ in His rightful place as King. It's the King of kings who's standing at the door, calling out to "the people of judgment" to hear His voice and open the door.

The word "witness," added to His title "Faithful and True," is revealing. The Greek word is *martoos*, from where we get the term "martyr," someone who is killed for his or her faith. Jesus, the Lamb that was slain, is the sacrifice for our sin. Christ's title, "the faithful and true witness" (Rev 3:14), carries on the "amen" principle of the total inclusivity of His nature and character by presenting the fullness of His three-part ministry for our salvation. For Laodicea, Jesus *was* the sacrifice, *is* the High Priest, and *will* become King. Jesus is all in all. Oh, what a Savior!

The third title of Christ given to the church of Laodicea, "the ruler of God's creation" (NIV), is the most obvious title of the three that directs our attention to His kingship. The word "ruler" is from the Greek *arche'* and can be translated "ruler" or "initiator, beginner." *Arche'*, from where we derive the word "arch," means "above all." Christ is exalted as One above all God's creation. This exaltation of Christ to the throne of the universe as the Creator is the "restoration of all things" (Acts 3:21, NKJV). He ascends to the very position from which He descended to save lost humanity.

The word *arche'* can also be translated "the beginning" (KJV) or "origin" (NRSV) of God's creation. Jesus's position as Ruler is beginning or initiating the final acts of creation that will end the conflict between the Creator and creatures over who is great. The concepts of ruler, beginner, and initiator are intertwined. For example, "In the beginning was the

Word, and the Word was with God, and the Word was God. The same was in the beginning with God. All things were made by Him; and without him was not any thing made that was made. In Him is life" (John 1:1–3).

Jesus is the *arche'* of creation. He is the Ruler, Beginner, and Initiator of creation. We recognized earlier that the act of creation is a kingly function. "I am the LORD, your Holy One, Israel's creator, your King" (Isa. 43:15). Jesus is the "I AM," Holy One, Creator, and our King. This revelation of Jesus, given to Laodicea in kingly titles, begins or initiates the final acts in the controversy that bring about the end.

The titles of Jesus at the beginning of the message to Laodicea are unmistakable evidence of the importance of His kingly ministry to His end-time church. The message also ends with clear and direct references to Christ's kingship and what that means to Laodicea. "To him that overcometh will I grant to sit with me in my throne, even as I also overcame, and am set down with my Father in his throne" (Rev. 3:21).

Every Seventh-day Adventists knows that Jesus moved from the Holy Place to the Most Holy Place in 1844, the time of the church of Philadelphia. This event began the antitypical day of atonement, where our Great High Priest is now mediating before the throne of God for the cleansing of sin. This was the position and work of Jesus in the heavenly sanctuary when the church of Laodicea came into existence. His titles as king at the beginning of the message to Laodicea and the statement regarding sitting down with His Father on His throne at the end describe a clear and obvious transition in the ministry of Jesus from High Priest to King. This Christ event happens during the time of the Laodicean church. How could the message of the transition of Christ's ministry from Priest to King be more straightforward and plainly spoken?

Further evidence that the coronation of Christ happens during the time of the church of Laodicea is evidenced in the council of the True Witness: "I counsel you to buy from Me gold refined in the fire, that you may be rich; and white garments, that you may be clothed, that the shame of your nakedness may not be revealed; and anoint your eyes with eye salve, that you may see" (Rev. 3:18, NKJV).

The three items of importance to Laodicea—the gold, white raiment, and eye salve—reflect the three emblems received by the king at his inauguration. The Bible describes the coronation of the boy Joash and identifies the three articles given to the king at his installation: "And he brought out the king's son, put the crown on him, and gave him the Testimony;

they made him king and anointed him, and they clapped their hands and said, Long live the King!" (2 Kings 11:12, NKJV).

The boy received the crown of gold, the testimony or scroll of the law, and was anointed with oil and proclaimed king. The connection of the "gold tried in the fire" to the gold crown of the king is obvious. In Revelation 14:14, the Son of man sits on a cloud with a golden crown on His head because He is the King. The connection of "anointing your eyes with eye salve" to the anointing oil poured upon the king is also obvious.

The "white garments" to clothe and hide her nakedness is connected to the scroll of the law given to the king because they represent the righteous acts of the saints. "And to her was granted that she should be arrayed in fine linen, clean and white; for the fine linen is the righteousness of the saints" (19:8). They are righteous acts because they are in harmony with and the expression of God's holy law. They "keep the commandments of God, and the faith of Jesus" (14:12).

The three emblems that Laodicea is counseled to buy from the True Witness are types of the emblems He is to receive at His coronation as King. Laodicea is being invited to give up on the "riches and goods" of the kingdom of this world and invest in the King and His coming kingdom. The kingship of Christ and the three emblems He receives at His coronation constitute the message and experience for Laodicea that gives them the victory and therefore the right to sit with Christ on His throne, even as He overcame and sat down with His Father on His throne (see 3:21).

The church of Laodicea began as a result of our Great High Priest moving into the Most Holy Place in 1844 and beginning the antitypical day of atonement. Laodicea's understanding of the judgement has centered around this high-priestly ministration. However, the description of Jesus given to Laodicea in His name, "the Amen, the Faithful and True witness, the ruler of God's creation" (v. 14, NIV), is a clear reference to kingship. This means that during the time of the church of Laodicea, Christ will transition from Priest to King, as was prophesied by Zechariah: He "shall sit and rule on His throne; So He shall be a Priest on His throne" (Zech. 6:13, NKJV).

He will begin the judgment process, starting with the house of God: Laodicea, people of judgment. The references to kingship throughout Christ's message to Laodicea are clear evidence to support this conclusion. The kingship of Christ is the message to Laodicea: "I rebuke ... I stand at the door ... I will come" is to awaken lethargic Laodicea out of her arrogant, lukewarm condition. "To the one who is victorious, I will give the right to sit with me on my throne, just as I was victorious and sat down with my Father on his throne" (Rev. 3:21, NIV). The message to the church of Laodicea proclaims in a loud voice that Jesus is becoming King. This is the spark that ignites into flame the message of the gospel of the kingdom to be proclaimed to the whole world.

The King is Be-coming!! The King is Be-coming!!!

Just a Thought #2

There are interesting parallels and specific connections between the seventh part of Daniel 7—the Son of man's coronation as King (see vs. 13, 14)—and our Lord's message to Laodicea (see Rev. 3:14–22), which go far beyond coincidence. Both describe the exaltation of Jesus Christ as King to the throne. In Daniel 7, the Son of man receives "dominion, and glory, and a kingdom" (v. 13). In the message to Laodicea, He "sat down with [His] Father in His throne" (Rev. 3:21, NKJV).

Both are in the context of judgment. The term "judgment" is employed three times in the prophecy of Daniel 7 (see vs. 10, 22, 26). Scholars recognize the "central concept of judgment"[61] in Daniel 7 as a primary theme of the whole book. Daniel's name literally means "God is judge." Likewise, the name "Laodicea" literally means "people of judgment" and presents Jesus as saying, "I stand at the door" (Rev. 3:20). According to James, "the judge is standing at the door" (James 5:9, NKJV).

Daniel and Revelation are classified as apocalyptic literature. One of the aspects of apocalyptic literature is the "symbolic use of numbers."[62] The numbers "three" and "seven" are significant in the schema of God's kingdom. The number "seven" is employed "as a mystic sign word" of "symbolic significance."[63] It is "a cardinal number; seven, as the sacred full one."[64] Harris agrees that seven signifies "sacred-completeness ... mark-

---

[61]Zdravko Stefanovic, *Daniel, Wisdom to the Wise* (Nampa, Idaho: Pacific Press Publishing Association 2007), p. 29.
[62]Ibid., p. 27.
[63]Laird Harris, *Theological Wordbook of the Old Testament* (Chicago: Moody Press, 1980), p. 898.
[64]James Strong, *Strong's Exhaustive Concordance* (Peabody, MA: Hendrickson Publishers, Inc., 2007), p. 1578.

ing the totality of a cycle or an accomplished task."[65] Three, also a prime number, mirrors seven as playing "a significant role in the Old Testament," as it "came to represent the smallest complete cycle."[66]

> *Daniel and Revelation are classified as apocalyptic literature. One of the aspects of apocalyptic literature is the "symbolic use of numbers." The numbers "three" and "seven" are significant in the schema of God's kingdom.*

The seventh part of Daniel 7, the coronation of the Son of man, is written in the pattern of seven threes. The message to the church of Laodicea is the seventh message to the seven churches, symbolized by the seven-branch lampstand of Revelation 1. This message is also characterized in its written form by seven threes. This mirrored pattern can hardly be seen as coincidental when the parallel themes of kingship and judgment, in terms of seven and three, are so evident. Both reveal the sacred completeness of God's plan of salvation in the enthronement of the Son of man.

Seven Threes of Daniel 7:13–14

1. Son of man/to Him is given/all should serve Him
2. Coming/came/was presented
3. Clouds of heaven (throne)/Ancient of Days/Him (God)
4. Dominion/glory/kingdom
5. People/nations/languages
6. Dominion/dominion/kingdom
7. Everlasting/will not pass away/will not be destroyed

Seven Threes of the Message to Laodicea (Rev. 3:14–22)

1. Three-part description of Christ
2. Three-part statement: Christ ("I") knows Laodicea's ("your") condition ("cold nor hot")
3. Three times, Laodicea says …
4. Three times, "But" Laodicea ("you") don't know …

---

[65] Laird Harris, Theological Wordbook of the Old Testament (Chicago: Moody Press, 1980), p. 898.
[66] Ibid., p. 933.

5. Three-part counsel to buy "so you can ..."
6. Three-part statement: Christ ("I") will do "and" Laodicea ("you") should do
7. Three-stage statement of Laodicea's overcoming experience mirrors Christs' three-stage overcoming

Chapter 10

Michael Stands Up

Any serious discussion of the final crisis on earth that culminates in the second coming of our Lord and Savior Jesus Christ must take into consideration Daniel 12:1. This crucial passage identifies "a time of trouble, such as never was since there was a nation even to that same time." Students of the Scriptures have long recognized this "time of trouble" on earth as a reference to the final crisis that faces God's people before Jesus comes. In His discourse of "the sign of thy coming, and of the end of the world?" (Matt. 24:3), after telling His disciples to study the prophecies "spoken of by Daniel" (v. 15), the Lord draws their attention to this key text: "For then shall be great tribulation, such as was not since the beginning of the world to this time, no, nor ever shall be" (v. 21). This is a clear reference to and restating of Daniel 12:1.

Sister White also referred to Daniel 12:1 in terms of the final crisis:

> I saw that the anger of the nations, the wrath of God, and the time to judge the dead, were separate and distinct, one following the other; also that Michael had not stood up, and that the time of trouble, such as never was, had not yet commenced. The nations are now getting angry, but when our High Priest has finished His

work in the sanctuary, He will stand up, put on the garments of vengeance, and then the seven last plagues will be poured out.[67]

What is the event in Daniel 12 that triggers the chain reaction to bring about the final crisis, great tribulation, a time of trouble such as never was? "And at that time shall Michael stand up, the great prince which standeth for the children of thy people: and there shall be a time of trouble, such as never was since there was a nation even to that same time: and at that time thy people shall be delivered, everyone that shall be found written in the book" (v. 1).

Based on the concept that repetition emphasizes importance, we recognize in the passage these repeated phrases: at that time (2x), Michael/the great prince (2x), stand up/standeth (2x), thy people (2x), and the description of the severity of the time of trouble, such as never was since there was a nation/even to that same time (2x). These repeated phrases are the concepts or themes that become the foundation upon which the meaning or understanding of the text can be established.

"At that time shall Michael stand up." This initial statement contains three of our repeated phrases and establishes their relationship. "At that time" describes the setting or timing of the event; "Michael" identifies the key figure around whom the event is centered; and "shall stand up" designates the event. From this core initial phrase, all the other phrases find their place to give the text its meaning.

Michael is the central figure identified by name and then immediately described again by His title, "the great prince." The event is embodied in the phrase "shall stand up." The event, to "stand up," is also repeated, but the second time, the emphasis is on the relationship of Michael to "thy people." Michael "standeth for the children of thy people." Somehow, the standing up of Michael cements the relationship between Him and "thy people" so that He has authority to deliver "thy people" from this "time of trouble, such as never was since there was a nation even to that same time."

"Whoso readeth, let him understand" (Matt. 24:15). To understand this text, we must first identify Michael and His title, "the great prince." This will give us some background and help to start identifying the event depicted: "Michael shall stand up." Once we fill in the pieces of who Michael is and what it means to "stand up," we should see the relationship

---

[67]Ellen G. White, Life Sketches of Ellen G. White (Mountain View, CA: Pacific Press Publishing Association, 1915), p. 117.

between Michael and "thy people," as well as Michael's authority to deliver, and also the book. The answers to these questions should make clear the event that sets into motion the chain reaction that results in the final crisis of this earth's history.

The name "Michael" means "who is like God." The Bible tells us that Michael is an archangel (Jude 9). The term *ar'-kho* in "archangel" means "to reign or rule over." Michael reigns or rules over the angels. In Jude, Michael is contending with the devil over the body of Moses. Moses, we know, was resurrected because he appears on the mount of transfiguration with Elijah, talking with Jesus (see Matt. 17:3). The apostle Paul gave us further insight: It is "the voice of the archangel" that causes the "dead in Christ" to rise (1 Thess. 4:16). From these facts, we can conclude that in Jude, the devil is contending with Michael over the resurrection of Moses. Michael overrules the objection and has power and authority by His word to give life to the dead.

Michael is not only the Ruler of the angels, but in Daniel 10:21, He is identified as "your [Daniel's] prince." "Prince" is the Hebrew word *sar*, which means "ruler," the same word used to describe Michael in 12:1. Michael is Daniel's Prince—*sar*—Ruler.

Michael is the Ruler of the angels and mankind. Because He has power and authority by His word to give life to the dead, He must be "the *Arche* of the creation of God" (Rev. 3:14). The title *arche* or "ruler of the creation of God" (NIV) is one of the titles of Jesus communicated to the church of Laodicea. The overlapping of the minute details in the various places in Scripture affirm the accuracy of the big-picture event that is about to burst on our world.

In Revelation 12, Michael is in conflict with the devil. "And there was war in heaven: Michael and his angels fought against the dragon; and the dragon fought and his angels, And prevailed not" (vs. 7, 8). The dragon is described here as "a great red dragon, having seven heads and ten horns, and seven crowns upon his heads" (v. 3). We notice that the term "great" is applied to the dragon here, just as the same term "great" is applied to "Michael, the great prince" in Daniel 12:1. The "seven heads" and "seven crowns" of the dragon of Revelation 12 are set in antithetical contrast to the "seven horns and the seven eyes" of the Lamb who is "in the midst of the throne" (Rev. 5:6).

The conflict in Revelation 12 is over who is great—the great controversy. Who has the right to rule? The "great red dragon" has "seven crowns upon his heads," claiming to himself dominion and authority over this earth. This is why he is enraged when the child is born "who was to rule all nations with a rod of iron; and her child was caught up unto God, and to his throne" (v. 5). Michael is the kingly name of Jesus Christ, the only One who is the rightful Ruler of humanity and angels—the Living Word of God. Only the voice of Michael the Archangel can give life "unto those who are dead" (1 Thess. 4:16). He is "the ruler of God's creation" (Rev 3:14, NIV), our God and King, the Lord Jesus Christ.

In the Scriptures, Michael is consistently presented as in conflict with the forces of evil. "Michael and his angels fought against the dragon ... and his angels" (Rev. 12:7). He is "contending with the devil" over "the body of Moses" (Jude 9). He is in conflict with "the prince of the kingdom of Persia" (Dan. 10:13). Here in Daniel 12, Michael is in conflict with "the King of the North," who is overflowing the countries of this world and even has entered into "the glorious land," overthrowing many (11:40, 41).

Michael consistently conquers the forces of evil and delivers His people. The dragon and his angels are "cast down" (Rev. 12:9), and the woman is delivered for the moment. In Jude, Michael triumphs, and Moses is resurrected, delivered from the prison of death and brought to heaven. In Daniel 10, the seventy years of captivity in Babylon are ended. The decree to set God's people free and return to their homeland is secured. Therefore, it's no surprise that in our passage, Michael delivers "thy people" (Dan. 12:1) from the King of the North, who "shall come to his end, and none shall help him" (11:45).

Daniel 12:1 is special for a couple reasons. First, all the other references to Michael and His victories over evil occur before God becomes a man in the person of Jesus Christ. Our passage is a prophecy of Michael's victory at the end of time, where He is Jesus Christ, the Son of man. It is also special because it directly links Michael's victory over the King of the North and His ability to deliver His people to the act of "standing up." Apparently, this act of "standing up" brings the great controversy to a cataclysmic, climactic end.

What does the text mean when it states that "Michael shall stand up?" The Hebrew word *aw-mad'* is used over 500 times, and according to Strong's, it is "a primitive root meaning to stand, in various relations (literal and figurative, intransitive and transitive)"—a common term to describe a physical position must also have a deeper meaning. "To stand" is also employed in Scripture in a figurative sense to describe a level of maturity, completeness, or ability attained to fulfill a position.

Daniel's book opens by introducing us to this concept. He and his companions are chosen by Asphenaz because in them, there was "no blemish, but well favored, and skillful in all wisdom, and cunning in knowledge, and understanding science, and such as had ability in them to stand in the king's palace" (1:4). The king is placing the Hebrew youth in school for three years, "that at the end thereof they might stand before the king" (v. 5). At the completion of the training, they are brought before the king. "And the king communed with them; and among them all was found none like Daniel, Hananiah, Mishael, and Azariah: therefore stood they before the king" (v. 19). Standing, in a figurative sense, demonstrates skill, ability, and understanding.

> *To understand is to "stand under" the circumstances, have discernment, and the ability to know what to do and be able to perform it.*

To understand is to "stand under" the circumstances, have discernment, and the ability to know what to do and be able to perform it. Throughout Daniel, "the wicked shall do wickedly: and none of the wicked shall understand; but the wise shall understand" (12:10). It is God who gives knowledge, wisdom, and understanding (see 1:17).

In many places in Scripture, the question is asked, "who is able to stand" (1 Sam. 6:20; Job 41:10; Rev. 6:17) or "who shall stand" (Ps. 24:3; 76:7; 130:3; Mal. 3:2). To stand, in the figurative sense, means to be faithful, have integrity, and the ability to fulfill whatever responsibilities are placed upon a person, demonstrating maturity.

The context of Daniel 12 gives us the specific position or responsibility under which Michael has the ability, maturity, and wisdom to stand. The Hebrew term *aw-mad,'* to "stand up," is not lacking in chapter 11. The phrase is used six times.[68] The overall concept of standing, either in the negative or positive, is used a total of eleven times.[69] The phrase in 12:1, where "Michael shall stand up," is the seventh time in the "stand up" occurrences and the twelfth time overall. These are the specific references in Daniel 11:

- "And now will I shew thee the truth. Behold, there shall stand up yet three kings in Persia" (v. 2)

---

[68] See Dan. 11:2–4, 7, 20, 21.
[69] See Dan. 11:1–4, 6, 7, 14, 16, 20, 21, 31.

- "And a mighty king shall stand up, that shall rule with great dominion, and do according to his will. And when he shall stand up, his kingdom shall be broken" (vs. 3, 4)
- "But out of a branch of her roots shall one stand up in his estate, which shall come with an army" (v. 7)
- "Then shall stand up in his estate a raiser of taxes in the glory of the kingdom" (v. 20)
- "And in his estate shall stand up a vile person, to whom they shall not give the honour of the kingdom: but he shall come in peaceably, and obtain the kingdom by flatteries" (v. 21)

Each time the phrase "shall stand up" is used in Daniel 11, it describes the event of someone becoming king (see vs. 2–4), beginning to "rule with great dominion" (see v. 3), or exercising kingly authority. This is the context of 12:1: "Michael shall stand up." The phrase "shall stand up" is in reference to taking kingly authority and beginning to reign. According to the context, Michael stands up when He becomes King and begins to reign.

Standing up is common biblical imagery regarding a king taking his authority and beginning to reign. In 2 Kings 11, the boy Jehoash is made king. "Behold, the king stood by a pillar, as the manner was, and the princes and the trumpeters by the king, and all the people of the land rejoiced, and blew with trumpets" (v. 14).

The Bible describes King Josiah's renewing of the covenant: "Then the king stood in his place and made a covenant before the LORD, to follow the LORD, and to keep His commandments and His testimonies and His statutes with all his heart and all his souls, to perform the words of the covenant that were written in this book" (2 Chron. 34:31, NKJV).[70]

Second Chronicles gives us further insight concerning our questions about the relationship of Michael to "thy people" and the book. The act of being king is described as him standing. This is alternatively described as "making a covenant." This same language is employed in 2 Kings 11, when Jehoash is made King. "And Jehoiada made a covenant between the LORD and the king and the people, that they should be the LORD's people; between the king also and the people" (v. 17). The establishment of this covenant is why the coronation of the king is alternatively described as a marriage. The king is crowned "in the day of his espousals" (Song of Sol. 3:11).

---

[70] See also 2 Kings 23:3

Both 2 Kings 11 and 2 Chronicles 34 also identify the importance of the book as part of the installation ceremony of standing up or becoming king. The act of the king standing means that he is taking authority and beginning to rule. Athaliah hears a great noise and comes to see its source: "When she looked, there was the king standing by the pillar according to custom; and the leaders and the trumpeters were by the king. All the people of the land were rejoicing, and blowing trumpets" (2 Kings 11:14, NKJV).

The standing up of Michael is the act of Jesus becoming King. Like Athaliah, the harlot of Revelation 17 will also resist the rightful King, but the news of this event will be trumpeted all over creation. The meaning of standing referring to kingship shines light on the significance of the phrase to Laodicea: "Behold, I [Jesus] stand at the door and knock" (Rev. 3:20). Michael standing up is the event of Daniel 12:1 that initiates the final crisis of earth's history. Jesus Christ, taking His rightful place on the throne as King, is the spark that sets ablaze the "time of trouble such as never was since there was a nation."

The Spirit of Prophecy affirms our biblical conclusion. In the upcoming quote referring to Daniel 12:1, Mrs. White connected the act of standing up to kingly authority: "When Christ stands up, and leaves the most holy place, then the time of trouble commences, and the case of every soul is decided, and there will be no atoning blood to cleanse from sin and pollution. As Jesus leaves the most holy, he speaks in tones of decision and kingly authority."[71]

Throughout our journey to answer the question about Jesus *becoming* King before He can *come* as King, we have looked at passages of Scripture that concern the time of the end to discern the events that must of necessity occur before the second coming. We have consistently found repeated references to Christ's kingly role as the major event in the consummation of the great controversy with the forces of evil. Is there any doubt left as to the validity of Jesus Christ our Lord becoming King before He *comes* as King?

The King is becoming!! The King is becoming!!

---

[71]Ellen G. White, Spiritual Gifts, vol. 3 (Washington, DC: Review and Herald Publishing Association, 1864), p. 134.

Just a Thought #3

The sanctuary serves as a miniature model of Christ's ministry and the plan of salvation. "Thy way, O Lord is in the sanctuary" (Ps. 77:13). The sanctuary is a pattern. The earthly ministration in the sanctuary is a type; the heavenly is the antitype. Could Christ's earthly ministry actually be a type and pattern for His heavenly ministry, one a mirror reflection of the other?

In the type, Christ's earthly ministry began with a cleansing of the temple (see John 2:13–22) message by Jesus, the prophet, declaring prophetic "time is fulfilled, the kingdom of God is at hand" (Mark 1:15). His earthly ministry ended with another cleansing of the temple (see Matt. 21:12–17) message by Jesus, the kingly (see v. 5) messenger of the triumphal entry, declaring, "The hour is come, that the Son of man should be glorified" (John 12:23).

Therefore, in the antitype. Christ's heavenly day of atonement ministry in the Most Holy Place began with a cleansing-of-the-temple message proclaimed by a prophet (Ellen White) and prophetic movement, declaring the prophecy of 2,300 days: "the time is fulfilled" (Dan. 8:14), the kingdom of heaven is at hand. Then, also according to the antitype, Christ's heavenly ministry in the Most Holy Place will end with another "cleansing of the temple" message by a kingly messenger, declaring, "the hour is come for the Son of man to be glorified" (John 12:23) or "the hour of his judgment is come: and worship" the Creator-King (Rev. 14:7; see also Isa. 43:15).

This type-antitype pattern is affirmed by Mrs. White's comments on the subject:

> When Jesus began his public ministry, he cleansed the Temple from its sacrilegious profanation. Among the last acts of his ministry was the second cleansing of the temple. So in the last work for the warning of the world, two distinct calls are made to the churches. The second angel's message is, "Babylon is fallen, is fallen, that great city, because she made all nations drink of the wine of the wrath of her fornication." And in the loud cry of the third angel's message a voice is heard from heaven saying, "Come out of her, my people, that ye be not partakers of her sins, and that ye receive not of her plagues. For her sins have reached unto heaven, and God hath remembered her iniquities."[72]

Since judgment must begin at the house of God (see 1 Peter 4:17), according to the type of Christ's earthly ministry, His heavenly ministry will conclude with a call to cleanse the temple (the soul, church, etc.), in the context of His kingship, in preparation for the wedding of the Lamb and His soon appearing.

---

[72] Ellen G. White, "Let the Trumpet Give a Certain Sound," The Review and Herald, December 6, 1892.

Chapter 11

The Midnight Cry

The "Midnight Cry" is a catch phrase known to Seventh-day Adventists from Christ's parable of the ten virgins in Matthew 25. Here, Jesus describes the final call given to the sleeping church to "go ye out to meet him," for "Behold the bridegroom cometh" (v. 6).

In the Midnight Cry of 1843–1844, early Adventists saw a historical fulfillment of these verses. William Miller's message of Jesus' imminent return and the call to prepare one's heart for the event swept across the United States in the late 1830s and early 1840s. The excitement grew to a fever pitch, and the numbers of believers swelled as Miller demonstrated from the prophecies the flow of history from Daniel's time down to the present day. According to Miller's reckoning, Jesus would come sometime in the year 1843.

After the initial disappointment of 1843, the Millerite Adventists saw in the words of Habakkuk a clear message from God: "For the vision is yet for an appointed time, but at the end it shall speak, and not lie: though it tarry, wait for it; because it will surely come, it will not tarry" (2:3). This carried them forward in their search for truth. It was during this time that they saw the error in their calculations and learned that the cleansing of the temple occurred annually during the Day of Atonement.

With this new light, the 2,300-day prophecy of Daniel 8:14 was understood as reaching down to the fall of 1844. The specific time for the fulfillment of the vision revived the former excitement of the movement, and it swelled into a "loud cry" message: "Behold, the bridegroom cometh; go ye out to meet Him." They believed Jesus was coming, and according to the Day of Atonement cycles, it would be on October 22, 1844. This series of events became the historic Midnight Cry, the calling card of the Millerite movement.

The "sweet as honey in my mouth" ended with "bitter in the stomach," as prophesied (see Rev. 10:10). Jesus did not return. The Bridegroom did not come for His bride. Hiram Edson, on October 23, 1844, was shown that Jesus moved from the first apartment into the Holy of Holies, beginning the antitypical day of atonement. With this light and other additional truths, Millerite Adventism blossomed into the Seventh-day Adventist Church, and the Midnight Cry of Matthew 25 became permanently affixed to the historical moorings of the movement.

The challenge for Seventh-day Adventists today is to perceive the benefit of Christ's teaching in these verses for our time. For some, the fact that the Midnight Cry is still to go forth seems to be forgotten. Is the Midnight Cry only a historical fact wedged in the annuls of Adventist history, or does it still have a vital role to play before the breaking of the day? Has the Midnight Cry of Scripture been fulfilled in our past, or must Adventism "prophesy again" (Rev. 10:11)? Mrs. White emphasized, "The power which stirred the people so mightily in the 1844 movement will again be revealed. The third angel's message will go forth, not in whispered tones, but with a loud voice."[73]

---

[73]Ellen White, *Testimonies for the Church*, vol. 5 (Mountain View, CA: Pacific Press Publishing Association, 1889), p. 252.

According to the plain teaching of the Scriptures, the writings of Mrs. White, and common sense, the Midnight Cry precedes the coming of the Bridegroom. This event is before us, not behind us. The command, "Thou must prophesy again," means, in part, that this final-cry message, taken up by the Millerites, must go forth anew with a significance of meaning as never before. "During the loud cry, the church, aided by the providential interpositions of her exalted Lord, will diffuse the knowledge of salvation so abundantly that light will be communicated to every city and town."[74]

For this to become a reality, there must be a significant revelation of truth that would motivate and empower the church to shake off the humdrum attitude of Laodicea and proclaim the message in every city and town. Is there more evidence within the text to shine additional light on the subject that will give direction and guidance for this most important event? To answer that question, we must, like the Millerites, go back to the Scriptures for ourselves.

The phrase "midnight cry" is not a verbatim quote from Scripture. The catchphrase is knitted together from the parable of the ten virgins: "And at *midnight* there was a *cry* made, Behold, the bridegroom cometh; go ye out to meet him" (Matt. 25:6, emphasis supplied). However, the origins of the phrase actually bring us all the way back to Egypt, where God is striving with Pharaoh to deliver His children out of bondage. The plagues have devastated Egypt, but Pharaoh stubbornly refuses to let God's people go. The Lord tells Moses, "I will bring one more plague on Pharaoh and on Egypt. Afterward, he will let you go from here" (Ex. 11:1, NKJV). Moses is sent to confront Pharaoh one last time, then he says:

> Thus says the LORD: "About midnight I will go out into the midst of Egypt; and all the firstborn in the land of Egypt shall die, from the firstborn of Pharaoh who sits on his throne, even to the firstborn of the female servant who is behind the handmill, and all the firstborn of the animals. Then there shall be a great cry throughout all the land of Egypt, such as was not like it before, nor shall be like it again." (Exodus 11:4–6)

Soon afterward, the Lord said, "On that same night I will pass through Egypt and strike down every firstborn of both men and animals, and I will bring judgment on all the gods of Egypt. I am the LORD" (12:12, NIV).

---

[74]Ellen G. White, "The Closing Work," The Review and Herald, October 13, 1904.

The term "midnight cry" originates from this judgment event. The Lord will go throughout "the midst of Egypt" at "midnight," and "there shall be a great cry." This is a final-judgment event that has both positive and negative consequences for the individuals involved. The negative aspect of judgment culminates in a closing of probation for Pharaoh and "the gods of Egypt." The firstborn of Egypt will die. The same event has positive effects for those who fear the Lord and listened to and obeyed His instructions. Not only were the firstborn of Israel spared, but they were consecrated to God and became the priests of Israel (see 13:1, 2).

The firstborn in the Scriptures is a symbol of kingship. "Also I will make him My firstborn, The highest of the kings of the earth" (Ps. 89:27, NKJV). The plague of the firstborn is a question over who is king—the gods of Egypt or Jehovah—and who is the true king's messenger—Pharaoh or Moses. Also, who will inherit the kingdom? The tenth plague of Egypt was the final call for individuals to choose their prince, his principles, and to which kingdom they would become subject.

With this background, we can see many parallels between the midnight cry in Egypt with that in the parable. First, we recognize that it's a judgment process; more specifically, it is a closing-of-probation process. The finality of the judgment is executed and cannot be changed. The firstborn of Egypt, as well as anyone not under the blood, surely die. Just as in the parable, those who are not ready cannot gain entrance into the wedding banquet.

Both midnight cries have to do with calling or coming out. Israel comes out of Egypt; the bridesmaids come out to meet the bridegroom. Both divide or separate the people to whom it is given into two groups. Both end up with one group able to pass over—leave Egypt—or enter into the wedding, while the other group is left in outer darkness. Both have versions of one group preparing, thus being ready, and the other group not ready. Both have one group saved or delivered and one group lost because both midnight cries have to do with the process of the closing of probation. Could both also be instigated by the question of kingship? With this background, let's reexamine Jesus' parable:

> Then the kingdom of heaven will be like this. Ten bridesmaids took their lamps and went to meet the bridegroom. Five of them were foolish, and five were wise. When the foolish took their lamps, they took no oil with them; but the wise took flasks of oil with

their lamps. As the bridegroom was delayed, all of them became drowsy and slept. But at midnight there was a shout, "Look! Here is the bridegroom! Come out to meet him." Then all those bridesmaids got up and trimmed their lamps. The foolish said to the wise, "Give us some of your oil, for our lamps are going out." But the wise replied, "No! there will not be enough for you and for us; you had better go to the dealers and buy some for yourselves." And while they went to buy it, the bridegroom came, and those who were ready went with him into the wedding banquet; and the door was shut. Later the other bridesmaids came also, saying. "Lord, lord, open to us." But he replied, "Truly I tell you, I do not know you." Keep awake therefore, for you know neither the day nor the hour. (Matthew 25:1–13, NRSV)

Throughout the history of Adventism, a study of the parable consistently turns into a discussion about the ten virgins. The dialogue, without fail, centers around what makes the five wise and the other five foolish. This personal application of the parable is not to be ignored or disparaged. It makes no sense to know about the end and not be ready for it. Therefore, without casting any doubt on the validity of that line of reasoning, one might dare to ask a most pertinent question: Are the ten bridesmaids—what makes some wise and some foolish—the point of the parable? It's a legitimate question, but how do we establish with certainty what the point of the parable is?

Well, there are a few literary clues that we can consider when trying to determine the overall meaning of any parable. First, we must consider the context. To whom is the parable spoken? The point of the parable must be relevant to those to whom it is given. Jesus, the Master Teacher, tailored His parables to instruct His audience. In this case, He is in a private meeting with His disciples on the Mount of Olives (see 24:1). This is something of importance to remember, but on its own, it doesn't answer our question. We need more specific information.

Often, when Jesus taught in parables, He would string a number of parables together; the repetition of the teaching would make His point clear. The parables of the lost sheep, lost coin, and prodigal son in Luke 15 would be an example of this style of instruction. Each parable in the series can stand on its own, but their connection reveals the overall point Jesus is teaching. This fact is pertinent to our study because our parable of focus is also one in a series of three in the Olivet discourse. Before we examine this series, there is another important clue found within the immediate context of the parable itself that we must consider.

Jesus often gave a clear indicator of His main point through a summary statement at the end of the parable, very much like a punchline at the end of a joke that brings it all together. This "punchline," sometimes given by Jesus at the conclusion of His parable, provides the key to unlock the meaning. This statement leaves no room for question as to the main point. With that said, does the parable of the ten virgins have a punchline that will help us determine the point of it?

In Matthew 25:13, at the end of the parable, Jesus breaks away from the story and gives us His punchline: "Keep awake therefore, for you know neither the day nor the hour." In this instructive statement, He reveals the emphasis of what and to whom He is directing the teaching in this parable. Jesus is telling His disciples to stay awake. At first glance, this seems to be in harmony with our past understanding of the main point of the parable, the condition of the ten bridesmaids, because they are asleep. Some awaken wise and ready; others awaken foolish and unready.

But wait a moment! The delay of the bridegroom caused all, both wise and foolish, to fall asleep. Therefore, being asleep has nothing to do with the difference between being wise and being foolish. All of our discussion about the difference between the wise and foolish virgins, however credible it may be at some level, cannot be the main point of the parable, since all ten sleep, and their sleeping has nothing to do with determining whether they are wise or foolish. The appeal to stay awake, therefore, cannot be addressed to the ten bridesmaids. Staying awake has nothing to do with making the wise virgins wise. Sleeping has nothing to do with making the foolish virgins foolish.

The punchline of the parable doesn't fit our common conclusion of its main point. The appeal to stay awake is not spoken for the ten bridesmaids, but if not, then for whom is it spoken? Furthermore, if the appeal to stay awake is not spoken for the ten virgins, then their condition is not the point of the parable. If we can identify to whom in the parable the appeal to stay awake applies, then we will understand its meaning.

It's here that the immediate context of this parable in the series can help shine light on our study to confirm the identity of its purpose. The punchline of the parable, to "keep awake," has been stated before. Jesus made the appeal earlier: "Keep awake therefore, for you do not know on what day your Lord is coming" (24:42, NRSV). The appeals are almost word-for-word. The repetition of the appeal confirms its importance and our conclusion that it is the fundamental point of the parable.

Between the two almost identical appeals of Matthew 24:42 and 25:13, there are three instructional vehicles, of which the parable of the ten bridesmaids is the third. The three parables cover the same ground, each adding to and expanding the instruction in a midrash style of teaching, the same style employed in the body of Christ's instruction to His disciples in Matthew 24 that mirrors the book of Daniel. To "stay awake" is not just the point of this one parable, but the overall point being taught by the series.

The first parable, about the owner of a house and a thief, simply states, "if the owner of the house had known in what part of the night the thief was coming, he would have stayed awake" (v. 43, NRSV). The main point is obvious. The second in the series (see vs. 45–51) describes the difference between a faithful and unfaithful servant. This, then, forms the immediate context of the bridesmaids parable and has important clues as to its purpose.

We will examine the parable in Matthew 24:45–51 alongside its sister passage in Luke 12:35–48 for accuracy and affirmation because Luke actually combined all three parables in the Matthew series into one,[75] which provides insights into their meaning. Together, these parables make clear to whom Jesus is making His point, which gives new meaning to the parable of the ten virgins specifically and new significance to the midnight cry within it.

> Who then is the faithful and wise slave, whom his master has put in charge of his household, to give the other slaves their allowance of food at the proper time? Blessed is that slave whom his master will find at work when he arrives. Truly I tell you, he will put that one in charge of all his possessions. But if that wicked slave says to himself, "My master is delayed," and he begins to beat his fellow slaves, and eats and drinks with drunkards, the master of that slave will come on a day when he does not expect him and at an hour that he does not know. He will cut him in pieces and put him with the hypocrites, where there will be weeping and gnashing of teeth. (Matthew 24:45–51, NRSV)

---

[75] The parable of the thief in Matthew 24:43 is in Luke 12:39. The parables of those in charge and the ten virgins are combined in Luke's narrative (see 12:35–48).

Jesus gives a parable about servants placed in positions of responsibility who are supposed to be serving their master until he returns from the wedding feast. Luke's appeal to "Be dressed for action and have your lamps lit; be like those who are waiting for their Master to return from the wedding banquet, so that they may open the door for him as soon as he comes and knocks" (12:35, 36, NRSV) directly weaves our two parables together.

These men of responsibility that are "put in charge" (Matt. 24:45, NRSV) are described as door keepers (see Luke 12:36), stewards of the master's servants "to give them their food at the proper time" (Matt. 24:45, NIV; see also Luke 12:42). These accounts mirror "the owner of the house" who is supposed to "keep watch" (Matt. 24:43, NIV) in the first parable. The faithful servant is a blessing and receives the same. "Blessed is that slave whom his master will find at work when he arrives" (v. 46, NRSV). The faithful servant is responsible to those put under his charge, "to give them their food at the proper time" (v. 45).

> *The unfaithful servant is not aware of the situation; the allure of evil has blinded his eyes. He puts off the event of his master's return and convinces himself there is still time to get ready. He is living in the moment, eating and drinking to get drunk. He is not only destroying himself but also neglecting those under his care.*

The phrase about the proper time for food is a curious one. Whatever the food at the proper time means, the faithful servant knows it and is responding appropriately for those under his care. Could we say that the faithful servant is sharing "present truth" with those in his care—truth that is pertinent to their edification and growth that will prepare them for what's ahead? The faithful servant demonstrates the same self-sacrificing love as does his master, and his master finds him "so doing when he comes" (ASV).

The unfaithful servant, on the other hand, gives in to the idea that "'My master is taking a long time in coming,' and he then begins to beat the other servants, both men and women, and eat and drink and get drunk" (Luke 12:45, NIV; see also Matt. 24:48, 49). He is described as an "evil servant" (Matt. 24:48, ASV) who knew the master's will but did not get ready or act in accord with it (see Luke 12:47).

The unfaithful servant is not aware of the situation; the allure of evil has blinded his eyes. He puts off the event of his master's return and convinces himself there is still time to get ready. He is living in the moment, eating and drinking to get drunk. He is not only destroying himself but also neglecting those under his care. There is no perception of proper time or food. He is totally oblivious to present truth and described as those whose lamps go out (see Luke 12:35). Part of the abuse suffered by those put under his charge is that they are not given the proper food at the proper time and therefore cannot get ready. The bridegroom comes at an hour they do not expect.

Jesus' multi-pronged appeal—"Be ye therefore ready" (Luke 12:40), "Keep awake" (Matt. 24:42, NRSV), "watch" (25:13, ASV)—to "whom the lord when he cometh shall find watching" (Luke 12:37), is specifically given to those doorkeepers who are given these positions of responsibility. The managers were to continually be in touch with the signs of the time, not drunk. In this prayerful watching condition, they would be awake and alert to give those under their care "their food at the proper time" (Matt. 25:45, NIV). Understanding the time, they are teaching others to build them up in the growth process (timing) so as to bring them to maturity, thus preparing them to stand before the Son of man.

The appeal of Jesus to stay awake is directed toward the managers in charge of the servants. Peter's response indicates he catches this sense and questions it. He asks, "Lord, are you telling this parable for us [the disciples] or for everyone?" (Luke 12:41, NRSV). Peter gets it. Jesus is not telling the parable to everyone; He is speaking directly to His disciples, specifically those whom the Master has placed in charge of His servants while He is away.

This is also the point in the parable of the ten virgins. The appeal to "keep awake therefore, for you know neither the day nor the hour" (Matt. 25:13, NRSV) is not spoken for the bridesmaids. It has nothing to do with the difference between the wise and foolish; they are all asleep. The appeal to stay awake is for the managers, but who are the managers given positions of responsibility in the parable of the ten bridesmaids?

The imagery in the parable of the ten virgins actually goes back to the sanctuary. This background will help clarify the meaning by identifying the different players in the parable. The Solomonic temple contained ten lampstands in the Holy Place (first apartment): "lampstands of pure gold, five on the south side and five on the north, in front of the inner sanctuary" (1 Kings 7:49, NRSV; see also 2 Chron. 4:7).[76] The threefold connection of the lamps, ten in number, in two groups of five, in both the parable and sanctuary could hardly be seen as coincidental.

The ten lampstands in the temple represented the ten tribes of Israel. Each tribe was represented by a lampstand (see 1 Kings 11:36), a table of the bread of the presence, and a laver. There were ten of each of these items in the Solomonic temple (see 7:27, 38). According to this imagery, the ten bridesmaids and their lamps represent the ten tribes of Israel or, in the New Testament context, the Christian church.

However, as we all know, there were twelve tribes in Israel altogether. We clearly see the five and five—lampstands and virgins—in both the sanctuary and parable, so where are the other two? Just as there are twelve tribes represented in the sanctuary, there are also twelve characters in the parable of the ten virgins. For both the sanctuary and parable, besides the two groups of five, the other two lampstands, or players in the parable, are positioned at the door or porch. They are the doorkeepers (see Luke 12:36) put in a position of responsibility over the other servants (see Matt. 24:45). The door was where the blood of the Passover lamb was applied during the plague of the firstborn in Egypt. The pillars of Jachin and Boaz are stationed at the porch (see 1 Kings 7:21)—lampstands of great size that represent the two remaining tribes that make up the twelve.

In the sanctuary, the pillar of Boaz was the emblem of the tribe of Judah. King David was the grandson of Boaz, the husband of Ruth. In the parable, the bridegroom is Jesus Christ, "the Lion of the tribe of Judah, the Root of David" (Rev. 5:5). Significantly, the groom in the parable is also the keeper of the door. When the door is shut (see Matt. 25:10), the "other virgins came also, saying, 'Lord, Lord, open to us'" (v. 11, NKJV). The bridegroom determines who enters in and who is cast out, because entrance is based on knowing him (see v. 12). "Behold, the Judge is standing at the door" (James 5:9, NKJV). Laodicea, are you listening? "Behold, I stand at the door" (Rev. 3:20).

In the parable all ten virgins sleep. Then there is a cry at midnight to awaken them. Who gives the midnight cry to awaken the ten? Someone has to be awake and accurately assessing the situation.

The twelfth and final character in the drama is symbolized by the pillar of Jachin in the temple (see 1 Kings 7:21), the companion pillar to Boaz. Jachin is the emblem of the priestly tribe of Levi. It is also positioned at

---

[76] Please see the diagram of the Solomonic Temple

The Midnight Cry

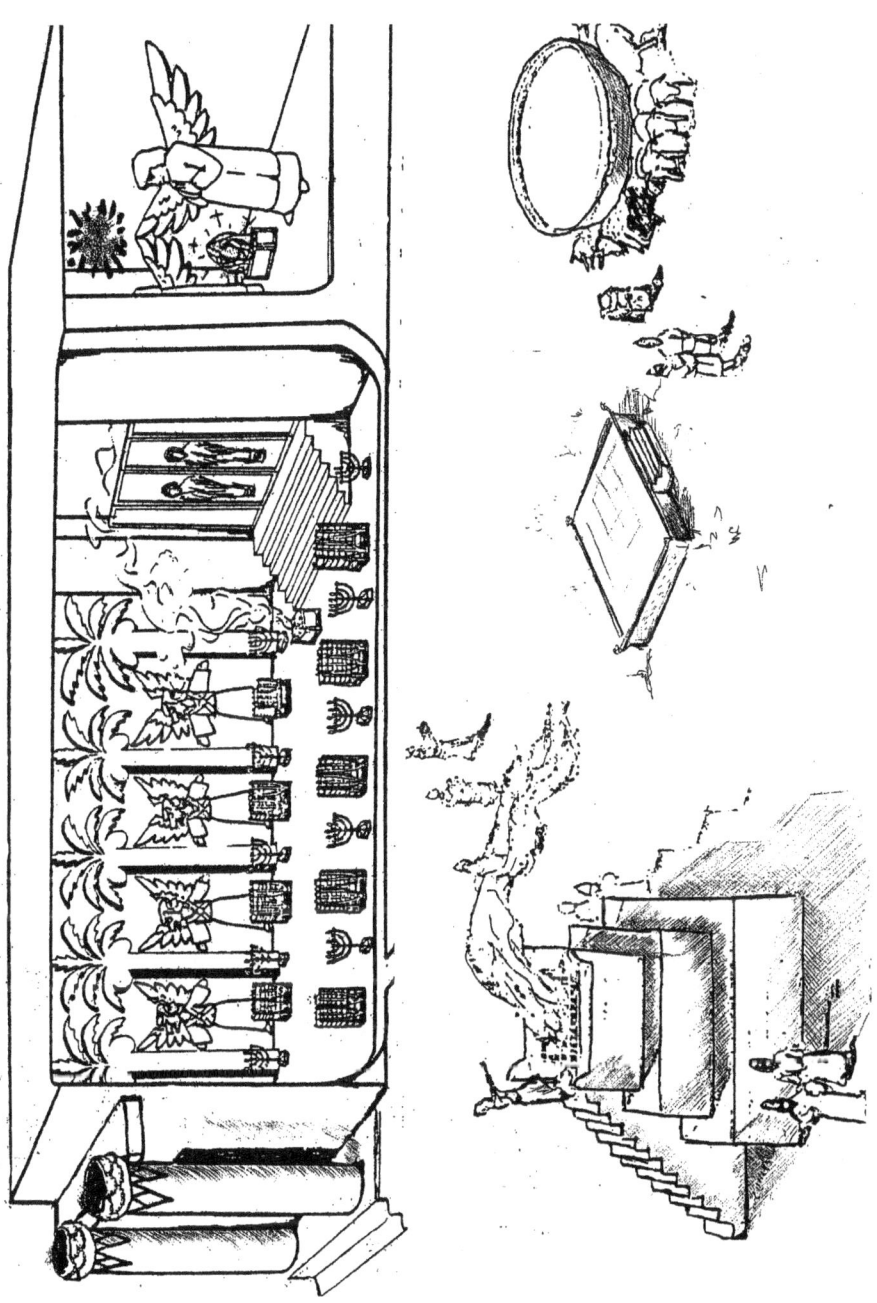

the door or porch of the temple, the place where the priests were anointed and inaugurated into service in the temple (see Lev. 8). The priests were given the responsibility to minister for the salvation of the people. It is the responsibility of the priest to prepare the bride for her Husband (see Mal. 2:1–7; 3:1–5; Joel 2:15–17) or "give the other slaves their allowance of food at the proper time" (Matt. 24:45, NRSV).

The priestly messenger from the tribe of Levi who is to prepare the way for the King or Bridegroom is the Elijah messenger. He is supposed to know the Bridegroom because he's "the friend of the bridegroom, who stands and hears him, rejoices greatly because of the bridegroom's voice" (John 3:29, NKJV). The priestly Elijah messenger doesn't know the exact time the Bridegroom will come, but he does know the temple liturgy and Scriptures. He is watching closely the signs of the times. He is able to give to others their food at the proper time and awaken them to the nearness of the time and the seriousness of the issues.

It is his responsibility to give the midnight cry to awaken the ten virgins. The appeal to stay awake is a warning for the Elijah messenger not to relax and become like the other bridesmaids. If the messenger that is to give the midnight cry and awaken the others is convinced that he is one of the sleeping virgins, then who will give the loud cry to awaken him? How will he know its midnight if he is not watching and waiting?

John the Baptist was this messenger at Christ's first advent. He was a priestly messenger, literally from the tribe of Levi (the son of Zechariah). He gave the loud cry message to awaken Israel for the Bridegroom's first appearing. John significantly describes himself as "the friend of the bridegroom, who stands and hears him, rejoices greatly at the bridegroom's voice." Jesus uses the same imagery to describe His relationship to John. "Can the friends of the bridegroom mourn as long as the bridegroom is with them?" (Matt. 9:15, NKJV). Jesus and John recognize and use the wedding imagery to describe their relationship to each other and the roles of responsibility that each has. The Elijah messenger, who prepares the way for the coming of the Bridegroom, is not one of the ten sleeping virgins. He is the messenger to whom this parable is addressed, with the warning not to eat and drink to get drunk, but to "stay awake."

The parable clearly identifies the players and their God-appointed roles, but what insight does this supply as to the message that would go forth with new meaning? The insight is wrapped in the wedding imagery to which the Elijah messenger is supposed to be sensitive. According to Scripture, the king is crowned on the day of his wedding (ref. Song of Sol.

3:11). When the bridegroom returns from the wedding to go to the wedding feast, he has become king. The kingship, the instigating factor in the plague of the firstborn that we saw in the closing-of-probation process in Egypt, is also mirrored in the parable of the ten virgins.

The clause "At that time the kingdom of heaven will be like" (Matt. 25:1, NIV) introduces the parable of the ten virgins. "The kingdom" concept is clear: "like men who wait for their master, when he will return from the wedding" (Luke 12:36, NKJV) is a reference to Christ becoming King, a fact that, to most of Christianity, represented by the ten virgins, is obscure. Our sanctuary symbol of the bridegroom, the pillar of Boaz, is the place in the temple where the king was installed (see 2 Kings 11:14). The tribe of Judah is, after all, the lineage of David, the heritage of the King.

The whole imagery of the lamp that the virgins awaken to light is kingly imagery (see 2 Kings 15:4; Ps. 132:7). The reign of Christ as King is directly connected to His wedding, "the marriage of the Lamb is come" (Rev. 19:7). The wedding is the coronation of the King (ref. Song of Sol. 3:11). The Midnight Cry is the call of the Elijah messenger that announces His becoming King. When Jesus returns, He comes as "King of kings and Lord of lords" (Rev. 19:16).

Mrs. White affirmed this conclusion in an amazing statement where she described the event of the parable, not as the second coming, but as the transferring of Christ's ministration from priestly to kingly:

> Jesus has left us word: "Watch ye therefore: for ye know not when the Master of the house cometh, at even, or at midnight, or at the cockcrowing, or in the morning: lest coming suddenly He find you sleeping. And what I say unto you I say unto all, Watch." We are waiting and watching for the return of the Master, who is to bring the morning, lest coming suddenly he find us sleeping. What time is here referred to? Not to the revelation of Christ in the clouds of heaven to find a people asleep. No; but to His return from His ministration in the most holy place of the heavenly sanctuary, when He lays off His priestly attire and clothes Himself with garments of vengeance.[77]

In this amazing statement, she was very specific as to the timing and event in the parable. It is not the second coming, "but to His return from His ministration in the Most Holy Place of the heavenly sanctuary, when

---

[77] Ellen G. White, Testimonies for the Church, vol. 2 (Mountain View, CA: Pacific Press Publishing, 1871), p. 190.

He lays off His priestly attire and clothes himself with garments of vengeance." She applies the call "behold the bridegroom cometh" to the ending of Christ's ministry as High Priest and transference to Him clothing Himself "with garments of vengeance." This is a reference to the very same event we witnessed in the prophecy of Zechariah, where Joshua the high priest, in the midst of his Day of Atonement ministry, changes his garments (see 3:4, 5) and is placed on the throne as king (see 6:13).

"Garments of vengeance" is a biblical phrase taken from Isaiah 59:17: "For He put on righteousness as a breastplate, And a helmet of salvation on His head; He put on the garments of vengeance for clothing, And was clad with zeal as a cloak" (NKJV). Here, the Lord is changing His garments. Why? "He saw that there was no man, And wondered that there was no intercessor; Therefore, His own arm brought salvation for Him; And His own righteousness, it sustained Him" (v. 16). What is His own arm? "Behold, the LORD God shall come with a strong hand, and His arm shall rule for Him: Behold, His reward is with Him" (40:10, NKJV). "His arm shall rule" is a symbol of his royal power. Christ has become King; it is the King who saves. "For the LORD is our Judge, The LORD is our Lawgiver, The LORD is our King; He will save us" (33:22, NKJV).

He is putting on his kingly attire in which he will go forth to repay people according to their deeds (see 59:18). "His own arm" and "the garments of vengeance" affirm the event of the coming Bridegroom as his coronation. Mrs. White placed these events and their timing as the context of the Midnight Cry, the beginning of the close of probation where all must pass before the King to gain entrance into the wedding feast. This Midnight Cry awakens the sleeping virgins to this climactic moment.

The message to be delivered is very specific to the sleeping bridesmaids: "Behold, the bridegroom cometh; go ye out to meet him" (Matt. 25:6). This is the Elijah message at the time of Christ becoming King. This Midnight Cry mirrors the original in Egypt because it initiates a close-of-probation process that will result in a state of deliverance for some and permanence of being lost for others.

Our purpose is in our name. The seventh day is the Sabbath, a call to worship the Creator (see Gen. 2:1; Ex. 20:8–11), who is the King (see Isa. 43:15). "Adventists" simply refers to His return. Our name essentially means "the King is coming" or "the return of the King." Since the Bridegroom is the King (ref. Song of Sol. 3:11), then "behold, the bridegroom cometh" is a legitimate explanation of the first angel's message. "Come out to meet Him" (Matt. 25:6, NRSV) parallels "Babylon the great is fallen ... Come out of her, my people" (Rev. 18:2, 4), the second angel's message. The separation of the wise and foolish into two groups—one saved, the other lost—rightly represents the third angel's message. "The King is coming" or "Christ is becoming King" is the Elijah message. This is the message of the Midnight Cry according to Scripture and the Spirit of Prophecy.

The parable not only identifies the players' roles, positions, and the message of those given these positions of responsibility, but it gives insight to the time of the loud cry and, therefore, to the coming of the bridegroom. Midnight is a specific time in the parable when the loud cry is given. The parable of the faithful managers also states that they give the servants their "food at the proper time" (Matt. 24:45, NIV; see also Luke 12:42). The specific time is important, "when he will return from the wedding," so the one put in the position of authority at the door, "when he cometh and knocketh, they may open unto him immediately" (Luke 12:36, ASV). All this evidence about timing also reflects the situation of the original midnight cry in Egypt and tells us the importance of the messenger not only understanding his purpose and message, but also the timing of his message.

No, we are not talking about setting a date for the close of probation. The message is not based on time because it is greater than time. There are no more time prophecies after 1844.[78] However, the friend of the Bridegroom who prepares the way hears His voice (see John 3:29) and understands the signs of the coming King and of Him *becoming* King.

Midnight is the hour, "when darkness reigns" (Luke 22:53, NIV). Who is the rightful king over this earth is the issue being controverted. When Christ is anointed as King in heaven, then "The kings of the earth rise up and the rulers band together against the LORD and against his anointed" (Ps. 2:2, NIV). The struggle is over who has the authority to reign as God and is thereby worthy to be worshiped. This was the same struggle in Egypt with Pharaoh and Moses. The kingship issue brings to maturity the conflict that began in heaven between Lucifer and Michael. The controversy now breaks into open warfare, but Satan cannot crucify the King this time, for He's being enthroned in heaven. Therefore, the dragon turns his wrath against the Lord's faithful witnesses on earth (see Rev. 12:17). This is the time when many of Christ's disciples will betray and abandon Him (ref. Matt. 24:9, 10).

---

[78]See Ellen G. White, Early Writings (Washington, DC: Review and Herald Publishing Association, 1882), p. 75.

The attempt of the powers of darkness to take kingly authority to themselves is a midnight experience for the world and the sign on earth that something has taken place in heaven. It is at this time and in this setting that the faithful messenger gives the loud cry to awaken the ten virgins. The messenger is himself awake to these things and gives the loud cry message to come out of Babylon and worship the true King. The messenger is responsible and gives the fellow servants "their food at the proper time" (v. 45, NIV).

The loud cry is the message of the revelation of the King—the right message at the right time, when the conflict over kingship and contrary decrees to worship are relevant to our world. The message, accompanied and empowered by the latter rain, awakens sleeping Christianity, symbolized by the ten virgins, to the crisis at hand. Some will awaken to shine light in the hour of darkness; others will awaken to be overcome by the darkness (see Dan. 12:2). However, the messenger will have proven faithful to his trust. The King is exalted.

Mrs. White connected the loud cry message to kingship in a statement that we previously read:

> "During the loud cry, the church, aided by the providential interpositions of her exalted Lord, will diffuse the knowledge of salvation so abundantly that light will be communicated to every city and town."[79]

The loud cry is empowered by "interpositions of her exalted Lord." The phrase "exalted Lord" can only be a reference to the final event: Christ being reinstated back on the throne of the universe from where he had stepped down to save humanity. He has become King. This event is the essence and timing of the loud cry message that "will diffuse the

---
[79] Ellen G. White, "The Closing Work," The Review and Herald, October 13, 1904.

knowledge of salvation so abundantly that light will be communicated to every city and town."

> At that time the "latter rain," or refreshing from the presence of the Lord, will come, to give power to the loud voice of the third angel, and prepare the saints to stand in the period when the seven last plaques shall be poured out.[80]
>
> This message seemed to be an addition to the third message, joining it as the midnight cry joined the second angel's message in 1844. ... I saw that this message will close with power and strength far exceeding the midnight cry.[81]
>
> And this gospel of the kingdom [King] shall be preached in all the whole world for a witness unto all nations; and then shall the end come. (Matthew 24:14)

---

[80] Ellen G. White, Early Writings (Washington, DC: Review and Herald Publishing Association, 1882), p. 86.
[81] Ibid., pp. 277, 278.

Just a Thought #4

The Chiastic Structure of the Parable

[Intro] "Then the kingdom of heaven will be like this.

> [1]—Ten bridesmaids took their lamps and went to meet the bridegroom.
>> [2]—Five of them were foolish,
>>> [3]—and five were wise.
>>>> [4]—When the foolish took their lamps, they took no oil with them;
>>>>> [5]—but the wise took flasks of oil with their lamps.
>>>>>> [6]—As the bridegroom was delayed, all of them became drowsy and slept.
>>>>>>> [7]—But at midnight there was a shout, "Look! Here is the bridegroom! Come out to meet him."
>>>>>> [6']—Then *all* those bridesmaids got up and trimmed their lamps.
>>>>> [5']—The foolish said to the wise, "Give us some of your oil, for our lamps are going out."
>>>> [4']—But the wise replied, "No! There will not be enough for you and for us; you had better go to the dealers and buy some for yourselves."
>>> [3']—And while they went to buy it, the bridegroom came,
>> [2']—and those who were ready went with him into the wedding banquet; and the door was shut.
> [1']—Later the other bridesmaids came also, saying. "Lord, lord, open to us." But he replied, "Truly I tell you, I do not know you."

[Postlude] Keep awake therefore, for you know neither the day nor the hour" (Matthew 25:1–13, NRSV, emphasis supplied).

Explanation of the Chiasm

The chiastic structure of the parable reveals its essence in the apex. The main point of the parable, in this case, is *to whom* Jesus is directing the admonition to "keep awake therefore, for you know neither the day nor the hour."

The parts of the parable are paired by contrast:

- In 1 and 1', there is a dynamic between the bridesmaids and bridegroom. In 1, they go to meet Him, but in 1', the bridegroom sends them away: "I don't know you."
- With 2 and 2', the five foolish bridesmaids contrast with the five wise ones who are ready to go into the banquet.
- With 3 and 3', the five wise bridesmaids that have oil contrast with the five foolish ones who are out trying to buy oil while the bridegroom comes.
- In 4, the foolish bridesmaids take their lamps but have no oil, while in 4', the wise refuse to share their oil: "No! there will not be enough."
- In 5, the wise bridesmaids take flasks of oil with their lamps, while in 5', the foolish ones request oil, "for [their] lamps are going out."
- In 6, "all become drowsy and sleep," while in 6', "all got up and trimmed their lamps."
- In 7, the essence of the parable is presented by the apex of the chiastic structure: "But at midnight there was a shout, 'Look! Here is the bridegroom! Come out to meet him'" (v. 6).

This portion of the parable portrays the timing "at midnight," which introduces our mystery player of the parable: the one in a position of responsibility; the friend of the bridegroom that somehow knows the right time and message. He's awake and aware of the current situation—what we might call "present truth."

While the ten sleep and are oblivious to what's happening in the world around them, this messenger faithfully gives those under his care their proper food at the proper time. When the time is right, he gives the "loud cry" to awaken the others: Behold, here is the bridegroom, who is the king (ref. Song of Sol. 3:11). Jesus makes his appeal—"Keep awake therefore, for you know neither the day nor the hour"—to the Elijah messenger so the faithful servant will give the loud cry to the sleeping world.

Awake, the King is becoming! Come out and prepare to meet Him!

Chapter 12

The Latter Rain

The midnight hour of this world comes when the "power of darkness" reigns (Luke 22:53). The scramble for authority and power "over all kindreds, tongues, and nations" (Rev. 13:7) is exacerbated because "tidings out of the east and out of the north shall trouble him" (Dan. 11:44). Satan hears the tidings that Christ is becoming King. In response, "The kings of the earth set themselves, and the rulers take counsel together, against the LORD, and against his anointed" (Ps. 2:2). The powers of evil confederate to rule on earth as a response to Christ becoming King in heaven.

In this darkness of midnight, there is a loud cry: the Midnight Cry, also known as "the loud cry of the third angel."[82] The message of Christ becoming King is to resound throughout the earth to awaken His sleeping church and invite all to the wedding feast. "At that time the 'latter rain,' or refreshing from the presence of the Lord, will come, to give power to the loud voice of the third angel, and prepare the saints to stand in the period when the seven last plagues shall be poured out."[83] How is the latter rain

---

[82] Ellen G. White, Early Writings (Washington, DC: Review and Herald Publishing Association, 1882), p. 271.
[83] Ibid., p. 86.

connected to the coronation of Christ in heaven, and what is its significance to God's people at the time of final crisis?

The Israelites were an agricultural society, dependent upon the ebb and flow of the seasons for their livelihood. In His wisdom, our heavenly Father explained the process of salvation through the natural cycles of the seasons familiar to His listeners. The temple liturgy, with its religious ceremonies and feast days, was directly connected to seed time and harvest, winter and summer drought. These practical realities were employed as symbols to teach deep truths of spiritual growth and maturity. "The Lord employs these operations of nature to represent the work of the Holy Spirit."[84]

The former and latter rains, so essential for the sprouting of the seed and the maturing of the harvest, became types and symbols of the pouring out of God's Spirit, so indispensable in His work of restoration in and for His people. The importance of the latter rain has been emphasized to Adventism through the Spirit of Prophecy:

> Those who come up to every point, and stand every test ... will receive the latter rain, and thus be fitted for translation.[85]
>
> The ripening of the grain represents the completion of the work of God's grace in the soul. By the power of the Holy Spirit the moral image of God is to be perfected in the character. We are to be wholly transformed into the likeness of Christ. The latter rain, ripening earth's harvest, represents the spiritual grace that prepares the church for the coming of the Son of man. ...
>
> ... without the latter rain to fill out the ears and ripen the grain, the harvest will not be ready for the sickle, and the labor of the sower will have been in vain.[86]

These statements stress the essential role the latter rain plays in the completion of the work in the last days: the formation of the image of "Christ in [us] the hope of glory" (Col. 1:27). This revelation of Christ in His church is a necessary prerequisite for His revelation in the clouds, to complete the gospel work and ripen the harvest for the coming of the King.

---

[84]Ellen White, Testimonies to Ministers and Gospel Workers (Mountain View, CA: Pacific Press Publishing Association, 1923), p. 506.
[85]Ellen G. White, Testimonies for the Church, vol. 1 (Mountain View, CA: Pacific Press Publishing Association, 1868), p. 187.
[86]Ellen White, Testimonies to Ministers and Gospel Workers (Mountain View, CA: Pacific Press Publishing Association, ID. 1923), pp. 506, 508.

> *The Israelites were an agricultural society, dependent upon the ebb and flow of the seasons for their livelihood. In His wisdom, our heavenly Father explained the process of salvation through the natural cycles of the seasons familiar to His listeners. The temple liturgy, with its religious ceremonies and feast days, was directly connected to seed time and harvest, winter and summer drought. These practical realities were employed as symbols to teach deep truths of spiritual growth and maturity.*

These references describe the importance of the latter rain, but the "how," "why," "where," and "when" of what the latter rain is has not been explained. Should something that significant remain shrouded in mystery? Perhaps an understanding of these questions surrounding the latter rain will give insight into the completion of the process ahead, making us more intelligent, active participants in its accomplishment. With that said, what light can the Scriptures shine on the mystery of the latter rain?

The former and latter rain symbols have been "mixed" in terms of eschatology because in principle, they are the same thing. Of the nine Scripture references wherein the latter rain is mentioned,[87] five of them (see Deut. 11:14; Jer. 5:24; Hosea 6:3; Joel 2:23; James 5:7) refer to the early and latter rains together as one and the same. God "has given the early rain for your vindication, he has poured down for you abundant rain, the early and the latter rain, as before" (Joel 2:23, NRSV).

This phenomenon is possible because both rains nourish the new growth and bring a harvest to maturity at the same time. The wheat and barley are harvested in the spring; and the oil and grapes are harvested in the fall.

"As the dew and the rain are given first to cause the seed to germinate, and then to ripen to harvest, so the Holy Spirit is given to carry forward, from one stage to another, the process of spiritual growth."[88]

---

[87] See Deut. 11:14; Job 29:23; Prov. 16:15; Jer. 3:3, 5:24; Hosea 6:3, Joel 2:23, Zech. 10:1; James 5:7.
[88] Ellen G. White, Testimonies to Ministers and Gospel Workers (Mountain View, CA: Pacific Press Publishing Association, 1962), p.506.

The rain symbols become interchangeable because, in principle and purpose, they are identical. Confusing at first, this insight gives us the surest foundation for interpreting the biblical symbolism of the latter rain. Since the early and latter rains are parallel and share the same meaning, the best way to understand the imagery of the latter rain is to study out the early rain. This is especially true since the specifics about the early rain are available because the symbol became a reality in a historical event. Therefore, in a study of the dynamics and conditions that brought about the experience of the early rain, we are in fact studying out the principles that apply to the latter rain.

The early rain event, recorded for us in Acts 2, came to pass during the Feast of Weeks in AD 31 at Jerusalem. Christians call this special event "Pentecost," from the annual feast upon which it occurred. This simple fact becomes the first significant thing to note. The early rain experience was not a random event but *is* directly connected with a set feast and temple liturgy that occurred annually.

The feast system, which gives us the timing, and the temple liturgy, which gives us the place, are symbols and types of the work of the Messiah for the salvation of His people. The feast system and temple liturgy as a "ritual service ... had been instituted by Christ Himself. In every part it was a symbol of Him."[89] In Christ and what we are calling "Christ events," the symbols become a reality; the types revealed antitypes.

This point is essential because the tendency of any study of the early rain is to focus on what happened to the believers in the upper room and the miraculous powers they received. However, without Jesus as the center, our perception of the event gets skewed. If we do not correctly understand the cause, we misunderstand and incorrectly magnify the results, and the essence of God's purpose slips away. Then later, when we try to reproduce similar results without success, we are at a loss to understand why. Jesus is everything to us; "Christ is all, and in all" (Col. 3:11).

Peter, filled with the Holy Spirit, affirms this truth in his Pentecost sermon (see Acts 2). The people at Jerusalem were, like us, in danger of attributing too much to the human element of the experience. Peter correctly directs their attention to Jesus. After speaking of Christ's death and resurrection, he states, "God has raised this Jesus to life, and we are all witnesses of it. Exalted to the right hand of God, he has received from

---

[89]Ellen G. White, The Desire of Ages (Mountain View, CA: Pacific Press Publishing Association, 1898), p. 29.

the Father the promised Holy Spirit and has poured out what you now see and hear" (vs 32, 33, NIV).

Peter fixes our gaze upon this exalted Jesus. The Feast of Weeks, or Pentecost, as an annual event in the temple liturgy, prefigured a heavenly event that literally happened to Jesus Christ in AD 31. Even without the specifics of what this means, we see that this is the essence of the Pentecost or early rain experience and the cause of the effects that we see fall upon the church. Christ, the head, is exalted and anointed in heaven. He receives the promised Holy Spirit, the "precious oil upon the head, running down" (Ps. 133:2, NKJV) to His body, the church (see Col. 1:18). The brethren who "dwell together in unity" (Ps. 133:1) receive power to bear witness to His glory and participate in the blessings.

> *Knowing the intimate parallel between the early and latter rains, we see historically that the early rain was a Christ event that happened in heaven, typified by a set feast and temple liturgy. Therefore, the latter rain must also be a Christ event that happens in heaven and is typified by a set feast and temple liturgy.*

Knowing the intimate parallel between the early and latter rains, we see historically that the early rain was a Christ event that happened in heaven, typified by a set feast and temple liturgy. Therefore, the latter rain must also be a Christ event that happens in heaven and is typified by a set feast and temple liturgy.

The fact that the temple feast symbol of Pentecost is an event that happens to Jesus Christ is affirmed by the two previous feast symbols that also became Christ events for our salvation. These events also occurred at the specific time of an annual feast and a specific place in the temple, according to the liturgy. The crucifixion of Christ is the antitype of Passover and features the altar of burnt offering in the temple courtyard where the sacrifices are offered. The Gospels present the death of Jesus as occurring on the very day. At the exact moment when the priest is about to slay the Passover lamb, the knife falls from his hand[90] and the earth shakes (see Matt. 27:50, 51), then Christ cries out "it is finished" (John 19:30).

---

[90]See Ibid., p. 756.

The resurrection of Christ is the antitype of the wave sheaf, which featured the offering of the first fruits of the harvest (see Lev. 23:10). The wave sheaf offering is presented "the day after the Sabbath" (see v. 11, NKJV), or Sunday morning on Passover weekend. The Scriptures, referring to the resurrection, describe Christ as the "firstfruits" (1 Cor. 15:20) from the dead. This event transpires at the very time the wave sheaf offering of the first fruits is offered at the temple, the day after the Sabbath.

Christ rises from the grave, and saints of old rise with him (see Matt. 27:52, 53) as the prayers of dew are offered at the temple. "Your dead shall live, their corpses shall rise. O dwellers in the dust, awake and sing for joy. For your dew is a radiant dew, and the earth will give birth to those long dead" (Isa. 26:19, NRSV). The laver of "washing of regeneration" (Titus 3:5) in the temple courtyard is featured in the wave sheaf and is the type of the death and resurrection of the Messiah. The NT boldly proclaims this type is fulfilled in Christ, so now those who become His are baptized into His death and resurrection (see Rom. 6:4).

Pentecost occurs seven weeks after the wave sheaf offering (see Lev. 23:15), and given the insight by Peter in Acts 2, we understand that Jesus is being exalted and anointed in heaven: "Exalted to the right hand of God, he has received from the Father the promised Holy Spirit" (v. 33, NIV). The earthly ministry of Christ as the prophetic messenger and suffering servant has been completed, and now He ascends to heaven to begin His priestly ministry in the heavenly sanctuary. "Now of the things which we have spoken this is the sum: We have such an high priest, who is set on the right hand of the throne of the Majesty in the heavens" (Heb. 8:1).

However, before that ministration can begin, in harmony with the pattern given in the typical service, the priest and temple must be anointed for service:

> And thou shalt anoint the altar of the burnt offering, and all his vessels, and sanctify the altar: and it shall be an altar most holy. And thou shalt anoint the laver and his foot, and sanctify it And thou shalt bring Aaron and his sons unto the door of the tabernacle of the congregation, and wash them with water. And thou shalt put upon Aaron the holy garments, and anoint him, and sanctify him; that he may minister unto me in the priest's office. (Exodus 40:10–13).

This event takes place at "the door of the tabernacle" or the porch of the temple (see Lev. 8:3, 31, 33), which features the right-hand (south) side of the sanctuary. As the porch of the temple is featured at Pentecost, where Christ is being anointed as our High Priest,[91] so the earthly extension of Christ, His church, also receives the blessing of the Holy Spirit and begins to meet for assembly at the porch of the temple, known as Solomon's Portico. "And by the hands of the apostles were many signs and wonders wrought among the people; (and they were all with one accord in Solomon's porch" (Acts 5:12).

In each of the first three feasts, we see an intimate and direct connection between Christ and His church. Each feast has a special place in the timing and liturgy of the temple in connection with Christ's experience, which flows down to and is reflected in the experience and message of His church.

A significant transition occurs at Pentecost. Up to this time, the Christ events typified in the temple feast liturgy have happened on earth in view of humanity. At Pentecost, Christ has already ascended to heaven, and He "must remain in heaven until the time of universal restoration that God announced long ago through his holy prophets" (Acts 3:21, NRSV). Now, starting with Pentecost and continuing with the subsequent feasts, the Christ events are beyond the sight of humanity and can only be deciphered by the evidence given from the Scriptures in the prophecies, temple types, and symbolic feast liturgy.

The feast system and temple liturgy as a "ritual service ... had been instituted by Christ Himself. In every part it was a symbol of Him."[92] Based upon this understanding, there is a specific action performed upon or by the Messiah that each feast, with its specific ceremonies, timing, and place in the temple, symbolizes. They typify an actual event and work of the Messiah in His process for our salvation. The festivals of the temple highlight this work by focusing the believer's attention on a specific aspect of the temple liturgy, therefore bringing to light new revelations of Christ's ministration. The church on earth is to follow, grow, and bring forth a harvest in connection with Christ's work for our salvation, just as the church at Pentecost did. "Till we all come to the unity of the faith and

---

[91]Specifically, the pillar Jachin (see 1 Kings 7:21), the pillar to the south or righthand side of the entrance. The right side is featured in the anointing of the priest (see Lev. 8:22, 23). Jesus is "exalted to the right hand of God" (Acts 2:33, NKJV).

[92]Ellen White, The Desire of Ages (Mountain View, CA: Pacific Press Publishing Association, 1898), p. 29.

of the knowledge of the Son of God, to a perfect man, to the measure of the stature of the fullness of Christ" (Eph. 4:13, NKJV).[93]

The connection between heaven and earth was affirmed again in the experience realized in 1844. After the Great Disappointment, the Advent movement on earth was discovered to be a result of Christ's movement in heaven, the great antitypical day of atonement. Christ moved from the Holy Place into the Most Holy Place, as typified in the earthly pattern (see Lev. 16) and delineated by the 2,300-day time prophecy of the cleansing of the temple (see Dan. 8:14). These truths kept Christ and His work of atonement in view, guiding the church through the mysteries of the Great Disappointment and giving needed direction and purpose for our work. From this same understanding and application of the principle, we can see the potential for an understanding of the latter rain to shine light on the future work of Jesus and the role of His church for the last days.

Knowing the parallel between the early and latter rains and the connection of the early rain to the annual feast of Pentecost, we are setting forth the thesis that the latter rain is also connected to a set feast, not a random event. We have seen that the feast system and temple liturgy symbolically describe Christ events that typify His work in salvation ministry. Both Pentecost and 1844 are antitypes that teach us that when something happens to Christ in heaven, a corresponding effect manifests in and upon His church on earth. Therefore, in studying the mysterious symbol of the latter rain, we are really studying a heavenly event that happens to Christ. We are trying to discover the mysteries of His salvation ministry in heaven before He returns. "Surely the Sovereign Lord does nothing without revealing his plan to his servants the prophets" (Amos 3:7, NIV).

Considering these things, what is the event symbolized by the latter rain that is to happen to Jesus in heaven that brings His salvation ministry to completeness and His church to maturity, making clear the full revelation of His love to a dying world for their final invitation to redemption? The only sure way to identify the heavenly Christ event of the latter rain is to study the evidence in the Scriptures.

In one sense, a Bible study of the latter rain is a simple task because there are only nine specific references (see Deut. 11:14; Job 29:23; Prov. 16:15; Jer. 3:3; 5:24; Hosea 6:3; Joel 2:23; Zech. 10:1; James 5:7). These references will introduce us to the biblical imagery employed to symbolize

---

[93]See also Ellen G. White, Testimonies to Ministers and Gospel Workers (Mountain View, CA: Pacific Press Publishing Association, 1923), p. 506.

the ministry of Christ. From these scriptures, a consistent pattern of evidence emerges that clearly identifies the event and the feast with which it is connected, as well as opens up a wealth of biblical imagery that shines light on the subject. Let's explore the scriptural references of the latter rain for evidence.

Job supplies us with the oldest reference, while Proverbs gives us the most direct statement. Each mirrors the other, confirming their application of the symbolism and laying the biblical foundation to unveil the mystery of the latter rain imagery. "In the light of the king's countenance is life; and his favor is as a cloud of the latter rain" (Prov. 16:15).

Job demonstrated the antiquity of the same imagery that is repeated and resounded in Proverbs: "And they waited for me as for the rain; and they opened their mouth wide as for the latter rain. If I laughed [smiled] on them, they believed it not; and the light of my countenance they cast not down. I chose out of their way, and sat chief, and dwelt as a king in the army, as one who comforteth the mourners" (Job 29:23–25).

The similarity of the references arrests our attention. Both references connect the symbolism of the latter rain to the king. More specifically, they describe the "countenance" of the king in terms of light. Proverbs says, "In the light of the king's countenance is life." Hebrew poetry fosters a repetition of thought in different terms. In this case, "his favor is as a cloud of the latter rain." The importance of the king and his latter rain is highlighted in both statements. The three components present in both statements are the latter rain/water, light, and kingship. Both reveal the absolute dependence of the people on the king's favor and the resulting rain for life. The imagery is intriguing and stimulates our interest to study further.

The correlation of the latter rain to kingship is affirmed in Zechariah as well. The prophet stated, "Behold, thy King cometh unto thee" (9:9) and described the extent of His "dominion" (v. 10). Furthermore, "the LORD their God shall save them in that day as the flock of his people: for they shall be as stones of a crown, lifted up as an ensign" (v. 16). He then appealed to his hearers, "Ask ye of the LORD rain in the time of the latter rain; so the LORD shall make bright clouds, and give them showers of rain, to every one grass in the field" (10:1).

Zechariah attached "the time of the latter rain" to "that day" (9:16) when "thy King cometh" (v. 9), and the extent of His dominion is made clear. Again, these verses place the latter rain in the context of light, "bright clouds" (10:1), and kingship (see 9:9).

Hosea employed the same symbolism when he pled with Israel to repent and return to the Lord so that He could "heal" and "revive us" (6:1, 2), for "if we follow on to know the LORD," God promises, "his going forth is prepared as the morning; and he shall come unto us as the rain, as the latter and former rain unto the earth" (v. 3). Hosea also combined the imagery of the latter rain with light ("the morning"). The kingship imagery is veiled in the sunrise-healing-reviving language, the same as Malachi 4:2: "Shall the Sun of righteousness arise with healing in his wings." The veiled kingship imagery in Hosea 6 is directly stated in 7:5: "the day of our king." Again, we see rain, light, and kingship.

The promise of the latter rain in Hosea is followed by the statement, "Whenever I would restore the fortunes of my people, whenever I would heal Israel, the sins of Ephraim are exposed and the crimes of Samaria are revealed" (6:11–7:1). From the context, it becomes clear that the latter rain and the light of the king's countenance bring opportunities of healing and restoration to God's people. However, Israel and Judah are rejecting the law of God and thereby the Lawgiver. In exalting another standard of law to rule the domain, they are exalting another ruler. Hosea went on to describe the specific abuses of Israel in doing so (see 7:1–16).

In this context, Hosea added an important element to our study of the latter rain. He used the phrase, "In the day of our king" (7:5).[94] This element is the beginning of placing the event in a specific time frame. "In the day of our king" is also translated "on the day of the festival of our king" (NIV). Jerome, in his Bible commentary on this verse, identifies this day as "the celebration of the king's enthronement."[95]

Hosea clearly associated "the latter rain" with the "sun rising" (6:3) and "the day of our king" (7:5). It's the same three-part association we saw in Zechariah, Proverbs, and Job. The significant contribution of Hosea is the additional connection of the latter rain and kingship with a specific festival that occurs on an established day. This connection lays a biblical foundation for the latter rain's attachment to a set Christ event that is connected to annual temple liturgy through a typical feast, "the day of the festival of our king" (7:5, NIV).

This festival event must also have a temple liturgy and ceremonies that typify the real event to come. The first task is to identify what is "the

---

[94]The Hebrew *yome meh'-lek* literally translates "the day of the king." The concept of this being a feast day is based on the idea that the King has a specific day. The parallel use of a day pointing to a feast can be seen in *yome kippur'*, the Day of Atonement.

[95]The New Jerome Biblical Commentary (Upper Saddle River, NJ: Prentice Hall, 1990), p. 224.

day of the festival of our King" or discover what feast in the liturgy of the temple features "the day of the King." The identification of the specific feast would give us the temple liturgy and ceremonies associated with it. This imagery could then be compared to the enthronement ceremony of the king for repetition or parallels to see if the biblical imagery employed to describe its meaning incorporates the latter rain imagery.

Zechariah again supplied the evidence that solves the mystery of what feast in the temple liturgy would answer Hosea's riddle of "the day of the festival of our king": "The LORD will become king over the whole earth. On that day there will be one LORD, and his name the only name" (Zech. 14:9, NIV). At that time, all peoples are called to "go up year after year to worship the King, the LORD Almighty, and to celebrate the Feast of Tabernacles. If any of the peoples of the earth do not go up to Jerusalem to worship the King, The LORD Almighty, they will have no rain" (vs. 16, 17).

This amazing reference not only gives us the specific feast associated with the installation of the King, but succinctly ties together both the feast and event with the rain imagery. "To celebrate the Feast of Tabernacles" is "to worship the King." Zechariah identified the feast that is associated with kingship and the event. The text specifically states that "the LORD will become king over all the earth" (v. 9, NRSV), which means He is not yet king when the statement is made. However, "on that day there will be one LORD, and his name the only name" (NIV), describing a time to come in which He will be installed as king—the day of His coronation. This evidence coincides with the "day of the festival of our king" (Hosea 7:5, NIV) that has already been identified by some as "the celebration of the king's enthronement."[96]

The Feast of Tabernacles (FOT) is the feast in the yearly system that features the king and celebrates his enthronement. Zechariah most extraordinarily wove the rain and light symbolism with the enthronement of the king into the tapestry of the Feast of Tabernacles. This evidence provides a solid, biblical foundation for interpreting the typical feast and the antitypical event connected to the latter rain. The latter rain will descend from heaven when Christ is anointed as King upon His installation in the heavenly enthronement event, the antitypical Feast of Tabernacles, just as the early rain descended from heaven when He was anointed as High Priest upon His installation in the heavenly inaugural event, the antitypical feast of weeks (Pentecost) in Acts 2.

---

[96]Ibid.

The enthronement ceremony in heaven, when Christ will be anointed and installed on the throne of the universe as the King of glory, is the antitype of the Feast of Tabernacles event. This conclusion can be affirmed by comparing the biblical imagery of the Feast of Tabernacles liturgy to the enthronement imagery. The combined evidence would place our conclusion beyond all skepticism. Is there a connection or parallel between the Feast of Tabernacles ceremonies and the enthronement liturgy?

The FOT was one of the three yearly feasts for which the Jews were required to assemble at Jerusalem (see Lev. 23:39). This random fact establishes a connection between Pentecost and the FOT because Pentecost was also a required assembly. This is interesting to our study because of the parallels between the early and latter rains. In eschatology, the study of end-time events, Pentecost is the time of the early rain; the FOT is the time of the latter rain.

"The Feast of Tabernacles was the closing gathering of the year."[97] The temple liturgy for the feast featured two main rituals: the light and water ceremonies.[98] These ceremonies were reflective of God's historic watch care in the wilderness wanderings and celebratory of the Lord's goodness in that "the sun [light ceremony] and rain [water ceremony] had caused the earth to produce her fruits."[99] The SOP statements regarding light and water affirm our conclusions are in harmony with the biblical evidenced we have discovered so far.

> *The enthronement ceremony in heaven, when Christ will be anointed and installed on the throne of the universe as the King of glory, is the antitype of the Feast of Tabernacles event. This conclusion can be affirmed by comparing the biblical imagery of the Feast of Tabernacles liturgy to the enthronement imagery. The combined evidence would place our conclusion beyond all skepticism.*

---

[97]Ellen G. White, The Desire of Ages (Mountain View, CA: Pacific Press Pub Association, 1898), p. 447.
[98]See Ibid.
[99]Ibid.

The FOT's overall motion is out of the temple. In the water ceremony, the water is poured out at the altar and flows out through the Kidron to the Dead Sea.[100] The sanctuary becomes the source from which the living water flows out. In the light ceremony, the huge bronze pillars at the porch of the tabernacle are lit, and the light shines out into the courtyard, symbolically representing the sun and moon.[101] Again, the sanctuary becomes the source from which the light of life shines out into the world of darkness. The flowing forth of the living water and the shining of light into the darkness figuratively ripen the fields of the world for the harvest. The Feast of Tabernacles is also called the Feast of Ingathering.[102]

These symbolic temple services connect the annual harvest with the set feast liturgy to give insight into the salvation ministry of Christ. Regarding the feast system and temple liturgy, the "ritual service ... had been instituted by Christ Himself. In every part it was a symbol of Him."[103] The additional connection with past biblical events shines further light on the meaning and purpose of the event. The symbolic services, the light and water ceremonies of the Feast of Tabernacles, are a reenactment of Creation, when light was brought forth out darkness (see Gen. 1:3). The chaotic waters and darkness that obstructed Creation were split to bring forth the realm of order (see vs. 6, 9) that was then nourished by a source of lifegiving waters (see 2:6).

The reenactment of creation in the FOT also celebrates the enthronement of the King. "Yahweh's universal Kingship and His power in Creation ... together formed an important element in the liturgy of the great autumn festival as celebrated in Jerusalem during the period of the monarchy."[104] This makes sense because the King is the Creator (see Isa. 43:15); working creation is a kingly function.

Ivan Engnell describes "the king as possessor and giver of the water of life."[105] Therefore, a celebration or reenactment of creation is a reenactment of the King's power and glory to decree light that conquers the darkness and slay the water dragon of chaos to bring forth living streams of water. Is this what Solomon meant when he stated that "the light of the

---

[100] See Ibid.
[101] See Ibid.
[102] Hayyim Schauss, The Jewish Festivals (New York: Schoken Books, 1996), p. 171.
[103] Ellen G. White, The Desire of Ages (Mountain View, CA: Pacific Press Publishing Association, 1898), p. 29.
[104] Aubrey Johnson, Sacral Kingship in Ancient Israel (Eugene, OR: Wipf & Stock Publishers, 1955), p. 61.
[105] Ivan Engnell, Studies in Divine Kingship in the Ancient Near East (Oxford: Basil Blackwell, 1967), p. 28.

kings countenance is life?" (Prov. 16:15). This imagery, although strange to us, is common ancient symbolism that God employs in Scripture to communicate amazing spiritual truth.

> Yet God my King is from of old, working salvation in the earth. You divided the sea by your might; you broke the heads of the dragons in the waters. You crushed the heads of Leviathan; you gave him as food for the creatures of the wilderness. You cut openings for springs and torrents; you dried up the ever-flowing streams. Yours is the day, yours also the night; you established the luminaries and the sun. (Psalm 74:12–16, NRSV).

The psalmist, under the inspiration of the Holy Spirit, described the creation of the earth as a cosmic conflict between God, identified as "my King of old," and a multi-headed dragon called "Leviathan." Again, the three elements of water, light, and kingship are front and center.

This greater cosmic struggle of light versus darkness at Creation is also reflected at the earthly level in the local, literal history of Israel. Therefore, the Feast of Tabernacles also commemorates the creation of the Hebrew nation. The King's decree of creation brings His bride out of the bondage of darkness (Egypt), leading them by the pillar of fire (light) by night and the pillar of cloud[106] (water) by day. The King in the cloudy pillar slays the water dragon of the Red Sea. In drying up the waters, He destroys the prince of darkness (Pharaoh) while He sustains the life of His bride in the Desert of Sin by supplying living water from the rock (see Ex. 17). God, the great Sovereign, frees His firstborn from bondage and creates for Himself a nation, according to His promises to Abraham, Isaac, and Jacob. This sounds just like the prophecies in Revelation.

The New Testament, of course, applies this typology to God's redemption from sin. In this sense, the Feast of Tabernacles is a multi-leveled event that commemorates and typifies the blessings flowing out from heaven to give life and light to this earth. "Happy are the people to whom such blessings fall; happy are the people whose God is the LORD" (Ps. 144:15, NRSV).

This is why Zechariah made complete sense when he cemented together the concepts of the Feast of Tabernacles, kingship (see 14:16), enthronement (v. 9), and rain (v. 17). There is no surprise then, that he, in the same context, referred to the light ceremony (vs. 6, 7) and living water

---

[106] The latter rain is described as "the cloud of the latter rain" (Prov. 16:15), establishing a biblical precedent as well as a natural connection between clouds and rain.

ceremony (v. 8), the two essential ceremonies of the Feast of Tabernacles, as events that happen to the King (v. 9) and have consequences upon the people in the form of rain (v. 17).

In fact, a significant body of biblical evidence demonstrates that the water and light ceremonies of the Feast of Tabernacles are consistently reflected in the enthronement-of-the-king imagery through the symbols of sunrise, dawn, and light, accompanied by images of rain, water, and river, "the enthronement festival being a new creation."[107] The latter rain references we previously noted are prime examples of biblical evidence that combines the water and light symbolism in the context of the king and affirms "the connection between 'creation' in the coronation ceremony."[108]

> In the *light* of the *king's countenance* is life; and his favor is as a *cloud* of the latter *rain*. (Proverbs 16:15)
>
> And they waited for me as for the rain; and they opened their mouth wide as for the latter rain. If I laughed (smiled) on them, they believed it not; and the light of my countenance they cast not down. I chose out of their way, and sat chief, and dwelt as a king in the army, as one who comforteth the mourners. (Job 29:23–25)
>
> As surely as the *sun rises*, he will appear; he will come to us like the early and latter *rains that water* the earth ... [In light of] the day of the festival of our king. (Hosea 6:3; 7:5, NIV)

In each of these references, the latter rain is consistently paired with the elements of light and kingship, but are these enthronement events? There is no contextual support in Proverbs or Job to substantiate such a claim. We did, however, discover the enthronement context of the latter rain and light symbols in Zechariah, when "the Lord will become king over all the earth; on that day the LORD will be one and his name one" (14:9, NRSV), and Hosea, on "the day of the festival of our king" (7:5, NIV).

Are there other biblical enthronement contexts that we can examine for similar imagery? There is no way to exhaustively address all the biblical evidence for the enthronement here, yet the examples chosen provide ample support to connect the Feast of Tabernacles water-and-light imagery to the enthronement and substantiate the connection of the latter rain to the coronation event.

---

[107] Ivan Engnell, Studies in Divine Kingship in the Ancient Near East (Oxford: Basil Blackwell, 1967), pp. 34, 66.
[108] Ibid., p. 201.

Psalm 110 is the most well-known coronation psalm. If the water-and-light imagery is intimately connected to kingship, then we should find evidence of it here. The psalmist, with the phrase "from the womb of the morning" (v. 3), skillfully wove together the birth and sunrise images to refer to the water-and-light symbols. The clause "thou hast the dew of thy youth" skillfully draws the birth, water, and anointing images together to reflect the water symbol.

The enthronement psalm ends with this strange yet now-understandable phrase: "He shall drink of the brook in the way: therefore shall he lift up his head" (v. 7). The exaltation of the king to the throne, the lifting up of his head, is associated with a reference to a brook beside the way. The dew of his youth refers to the anointing of the king and the lifegiving water flowing out to his domain. A drink from the stream beside the way is an alternate symbol of the living water, or the water ceremony that reflects the connection of the feast to the king and his new place of authority, which has positive and negative results based on one's relationship to him.

Micah also used water and light imagery to describe the coming King. The "dew from the LORD, as the showers upon the grass" (5:7) is in the context of the truth that "The LORD shall reign over them in mount Zion" (4:7). "And he shall stand and feed in the strength of the LORD, in the majesty of the name of the LORD his God; and they shall abide: for now shall he be great unto the ends of the earth" (5:4).

At the installation of the new King, "the LORD shall be a light unto me. I will bear the indignation of the LORD, because I have sinned against him, until he plead my cause, and execute judgment for me: he will bring me forth to the light, and I shall behold his righteousness" (7:8, 9). We know these references speak of installation because it uses the future tense: "he will reign," "he shall stand," and "he shall be great" (4:7, 5:4). Again, water-and-light symbols accompany the installation of the King.

In Psalm 148, the phrase "Praise ye him, sun and moon" (v. 3) is joined to "Praise him ... ye waters that be above the heavens" (v. 4). The water-and-light imagery is again in the context of the enthronement: "He also exalteth the horn of his people" (v. 14). This reference is significant because the horn symbol is literally dripping with imagery. The symbol of the horn refers to a king (see Dan. 8:21, Rev. 17:12), specifically the Messiah (see Luke 1:69) or Anointed One. The King is anointed with a horn of oil (see 1 Sam. 16:1, 13; 1 Kings 1:39).

The horn also is connected to light imagery: "I will cause a horn to sprout up for David; I have prepared a lamp for my anointed one" (Ps.

132:17, NRSV). The point is that Psalm 148 combines the water and light images in the context of exalting the horn, the newly installed King.

The pre-temple precedent of the coronation of Solomon by King David gives great insight into the symbolism and mindset behind it. King David gave very specific instructions for this event: "Take with you the servants of your lord, and have Solomon my son ride on my own mule, and take him down to Gihon" (1 Kings 1:33, NKJV). Gihon is a spring "located south of Jerusalem on the western side of the Kidron Valley."[109] In the absence of the temple, David has Solomon brought to a spring as the location of the coronation. "There let Zadok the priest and Nathan the prophet anoint him King over Israel" (v. 34).

This coronation ritual exactly coincides with the water ceremony performed in the temple at the Feast of Tabernacles, described here by Mrs. White: The water ceremony was "the most impressive ceremony of the feast, one that called forth the greatest rejoicing ... the priests dipped from the flowing waters of the Kedron a flagon of water, and, lifting it on high, while the trumpets were sounding, he ascended the broad steps of the temple." The water was then poured out at the altar and "flowed into a pipe which communicated with the Kedron, and was conducted to the Dead Sea."[110]

The coronation ceremony at the Gihon Spring, which flows through the Kidron, was replicated in the water ceremony at the Feast of Tabernacles. The two instances commemorate the same event. The symbolism of Gihon as the place of enthronement actually reenacts Creation and takes us all the way back to the Garden of Eden. Gihon is the name of the second branch of the river of life that flows out of the garden (see Gen. 2:13). Revelation describes the river of life as flowing out of the throne (see 22:1–3).

The enthronement of Solomon, occurring in the context of the Gihon, and the river of life flowing out of the throne are no coincidence. The connection of this imagery to the Feast of Tabernacles ties the two events back to Creation as well as forward to the final restoration of Revelation 22, confirming Engnell's conclusion that "in the New Year enthronement festival ... the act of creation is symbolically rendered"[111] These connec-

---

[109]The Harper Collins Study Bible, footnote for Gihon, 1 Kings 1:33.
[110]Ellen G. White, The Desire of Ages (Mountain View, CA: Pacific Press Pub Association, 1898), pp. 448, .
[111]Ivan Engnell, Studies in Divine Kingship in the Ancient Near East (Oxford: Basil Blackwell, 1967), p. 32.

tions reveal the ancient mindset symbolized in the enthronement imagery. The installation of the king brings the waters of life to a dry and thirsty land to restore the world of sin and death to its Edenic state.

This is the imagery that Isaiah employed to describe the event in this context of:

> "Now I will rise, says the LORD; "Now I will be exalted, Now I will lift Myself up." ... Your eyes will see the King in His beauty ... Look upon Zion, the city of our appointed feasts; Your eyes will see Jerusalem, a quiet home, a tabernacle *that* will not be taken down ... But there the majestic LORD *will* be for us a place of broad rivers *and* streams ... For ... The LORD is our King. (Isaiah 33:10, 17, 20–22, NKJV).

This will result in the parched land (see 35:1) and burning sand (v. 7) becoming a place of pools and bubbling springs. This is Isaiah's "Highway of Holiness" (v. 8, NKJV) where he described the restoration of God's image in humanity. Again, the Scriptures weave together the imagery of the enthronement of the King with a festival and living waters that bring this recreation and restoration.

This eschatological restoration is also brought to view in Ezekiel 47, where living water flows from the threshold of the temple down through the Kidron to the Dead Sea, giving life to all it touches. The rebuilding of the Ezekiel temple and the ensuing flow of living water occur in the context of a King (see 46:2) that unites Judah and Israel into one kingdom (see 37:22). The King not only unites all of Israel, but gathers her scattered children from all over the world.

The harvest gathering of Israel, the building of the new temple, and the river of life that flows from it are all elements reflected in the Feast of Tabernacles imagery. This passage is an obvious reference to the water ceremony at this feast, when the priest pours out the water at the base of the altar and the water is conducted through pipes down through the Kidron Valley to the Dead Sea. Again, the enthronement of the King is the time of the eschatological recreation, the antitypical Feast of Tabernacles.

Psalm 72 is a royal psalm that describes the enthronement. God transfers authority to His son, whom He is making King: "Endow the king with your justice O God, the royal son with your righteousness" (v. 1, NIV). It goes on to describe those things the King will do when He receives this authority: He will judge (see v. 2), defend and save the oppressed and crush the oppressor (v. 4), endure (v. 5), rule (v. 8), deliver (v. 12), take pity (v. 13), and rescue (v. 14).

In the midst of describing the attributes, characteristics, and function of the new King is this statement: "May he be like rain falling on a mowed field, like showers watering the earth" (v. 6). The coronation of the new King is likened to "rain falling" and "showers watering the earth." In harmony with the water imagery from the Feast of Tabernacles, the psalm also describes the King in terms of light: "May he endure as long as the sun, as long as the moon, throughout all generations (v. 5). Also, "May his name endure forever; may it continue as long as the sun" (v. 17). Again, the King's enthronement is described in terms of the imagery of the Feast of Tabernacles—water and light that bring life.

Furthermore, as the psalm declares, when the Son is enthroned as king, the individuals within the domain must take a stance one way or the other: Either they bow down and worship, acknowledging the new King, and become conformed to Him as the standard of all truth and justice (see vs. 8–11), or they rise up in rebellion against Him and declare that they have a more complete concept of order, thereby make themselves kings. These rebels become "oppressors" that will be crushed by the newly installed King (v. 4).

> *The exaltation of the Son as King brings the individuals within the domain to a place of decision or judgment, and therefore maturity, as to their relationship with God and His Anointed One. The ancients correctly associated this bringing of the harvest to maturity, one way or the other, with the latter rain.*

The exaltation of the Son as King brings the individuals within the domain to a place of decision or judgment, and therefore maturity, as to their relationship with God and His Anointed One. The ancients correctly associated this bringing of the harvest to maturity, one way or the other, with the latter rain. Thus, it is easy to understand why the Scriptures would say, "In the light of the king's countenance is life; and his favor is as a cloud of the latter rain" (Prov. 16:15). It also becomes clear why Zechariah would say, "Ask ye of the LORD rain in the time of the latter rain; so the LORD shall make bright clouds, and give them showers of rain" (10:1) in the context of "your King cometh unto thee" (9:9). The harvest imagery associated with both the installation of the new King and the Feast of Tabernacles confirms once again the connection of the two events.

The biblical imagery surrounding the enthronement of the King, together with the usage of the latter rain, affirms our previous conclusion. The latter rain is a symbol from a set feast—the Feast of Tabernacles—a symbolic temple liturgy—the water ceremony—which typifies a specific Christ event—His enthronement as King.

However, we still have some unexplored scriptural references to the latter rain. How do they fit? The worship of the king on the day of his coronation is critical because this becomes the moment that the subjects of the realm accept or reject the one placed on the throne. Remember the account of Rehoboam, the son of Solomon, who took for granted the kingship and the people? He rejected the advice of the elders to respond favorably. When he responded harshly, the people rejected him as their king (see 1 Kings 12).

The act of worshiping the new king is a ratification of the covenant between the parties that each acknowledge and accept the new conditions of the domain. The people accept or rebel against the king; the king accepts the people or casts them out (i.e., execution) of the realm. Adonijah, Solomon's older brother, is an excellent example of this principle (see 1 Kings 2).

When Solomon was inaugurated as king, the people "bowed down their heads and worshiped the LORD, and the king" (1 Chron. 29:20). This reference is peculiar because the king is worshiped along with or even as Yahweh. This strange incident occurs at the coronation of the son of David. The point is that the reference to worshiping the king has a historical precedent of alluding to the day of his coronation and establishes the covenant relationship. Continual or annual worship, going up to Jerusalem year after year to venerate the king and celebrate the Feast of Tabernacles (see Zech. 14:16), is a way to commemorate or renew the original covenant.

Every year, subjugated people, people of the domain conquered by the new king, must renew the covenant to maintain the relationship. Historically, for example, the Israelites had to pay a yearly tribute to Nebuchadnezzar to maintain the covenant agreement between them. In Jeremiah's time, they decided to break ties with Babylon and turn to Egypt. This act of rejecting Nebuchadnezzar as their sovereign was communicated by withholding the yearly tribute. Therefore, the covenant must be renewed yearly to be legitimate. The Spirit of Prophecy portrays this same "tribute to the King" sentiment to describe the FOT: "All brought some gift as a tribute of thanksgiving to Him who had crowned the year with His goodness, and made His paths drop fatness."[112]

Each year, the act of "going up to worship" is a rehearsal and acknowledgment of the enthronement of the king and the ratification of the covenant stipulations. This is the event being described by the phrase "Herod's birthday" (Matt. 14:6; Mark 6:21). It's not a birthday party for the day he was physically born, like we think; it is a celebration, recapitulation, or renewing of the covenant of the day he was crowned king. He was symbolically "born" on the day of his coronation. This explains the imagery in Psalm 110: "from the womb of the morning, thou hast the dew of thy youth" (v. 3); and Psalm 2: "the LORD hath said unto me, Thou art my Son; this day have I begotten thee" (v. 7). This symbolism is also present in Revelation 12 when the child is born, "who was to rule all nations with a rod of iron" and is "caught up unto God, and to his throne" (v. 5).

The worship of the king brings blessings; the rejection of the king brings curses. The blessings associated with worshipping the king are described in Job and Proverbs as "the light of the king's countenance" being like "the latter rain." They are depicted in the negative in Zechariah: Those who do not go up "to worship the King" at the Feast of Tabernacles "will have no rain" (14:16, 17).

The worship-of-the-king connection to the rain is illuminating. This imagery is based on the ancient understanding that the king is the stability of the realm (see Isa. 33:6). As mentioned already, the ancients viewed "the king as possessor and giver of the water of life."[113] Everything that sustains the welfare of the subjects within the realm and maintains the order of the domain comes from and flows out of the king. Nebuchadnezzar, for example, is depicted as a tree that nourished and fed all the creatures in his realm (see Dan. 4:20–22).[114] As an agricultural society in a climate where their very existence depends on the rains, the

---

[112]Ellen G. White, The Desire of Ages (Mountain View, CA: Pacific Press Publishing Association, 189), p. 448.

[113]Ivan Engnell, Studies in Divine Kingship in the Ancient Near East (Oxford, Basil Blackwell, 1967), p. 28.

[114]The tree symbolism is also very much a part of the Feat of Tabernacles because trees are another symbol of the king.

king who represents and acts for the deity would become the source responsible for those rains.

As an integral part of the coronation ceremony, the covenant is established between the king and *his* Sovereign, the Lord. Then another covenant is made between the king and the people (see 2 Kings 11:17). This establishing of the covenants typified a marriage: the king as the groom, the people as the bride, and God conducting the wedding. For the people to have access to the privileges and blessings of the covenant, they must remain faithful to their king.

In an agricultural society, the imagery employed to describe the covenant is connected to rain provided because of faithfulness to the covenant and rain withheld because of unfaithfulness. Moses spoke of the promise: "If you will only heed his every commandment that I am commanding you today- loving the LORD your God, and serving him with all your heart and with all your soul- then he will give the rain for your land in its season, the early rain and the latter rain, and you will gather in your grain, your wine, and your oil" (Deut. 11:13, 14, NRSV).

Jeremiah, on the other hand, promised the withholding of the latter rain blessing if the Israelites were not faithful: "Thou has polluted the land with thy whoredoms and with thy wickedness. Therefore the showers have been withholden, and there hath been no latter rain" (3:2, 3); "Neither say they in their heart, Let us now fear the LORD our God, that giveth rain, both the former and the latter, in his season: he reserveth unto us the appointed weeks of harvest. Your iniquities have turned away these things, and your sins have withholden good things from you" (5:24, 25).

James referred to the same covenant type of agreement in the context of the harvest as he appealed to his hearers to be faithful as they patiently waited for the coming of the Lord—patient like the farmer who waits for the early and latter rains (see 5:17). The giving or withholding of the latter rain becomes a consequence of the faithfulness or lack thereof to the stipulations of the covenant.

This summation of the last three of our latter rain Scripture references actually brings us full-circle to confirm Zechariah's witness. When "the LORD shall be king over all the earth" (14:9), "living waters shall go out from Jerusalem" (v. 8) and "there shall be continuous day (v. 7, NRSV). These are blessings to the faithful. However, for those who refuse to go up and worship the king, "upon them shall be no rain" (v. 17); "there shall be the plague, wherewith the LORD will smite the heathen that come not up to keep the feast of tabernacles" (v. 18).

Having searched all nine biblical references of the latter rain, the evidence is consistent and overwhelming. The symbolism of the latter rain is intimately woven into the fabric of the enthronement of the King. Our study focused on the water imagery, which led us see that both the light and water images of the Feast of Tabernacles are bound by Scripture to the coronation of the newly installed King. This imagery is consistent with our traditional understanding of events that must occur before Christ's return as King.

Adventists have long awaited the outpouring of the latter rain. This end-time event is associated with the mighty angel of Revelation 18 that comes to enlighten the earth with his glory. Our study places these events in the larger context of the water and light ceremonies of temple liturgy as consequences of the Christ event, the enthronement of the King.

The imagery of the latter rain is consistent with the symbolism of the early rain. It is not a random event that sporadically occurs, but an earthly manifestation of a specific heavenly event that occurs at a specific time as an antitype of a typical temple service ritual. In this sense, the latter rain exactly parallels the early rain. Just as the early rain was the anointing and exaltation of Christ as High Priest in heaven at Pentecost, which spilled over to become the outpouring of the Holy Spirit onto the apostolic church that began the gospel work, the latter rain is the anointing and exaltation of Christ in heaven as King at the Feast of Tabernacles, which spills over to become the outpouring of the Holy Spirit onto the last-day saints to bring to close the gospel work.

Both the early and latter rain events are manifested by the outpouring of the Holy Spirit onto Christ's church on earth, which is divine communication that an event has taken place in heaven. Notice how Mrs. White also associated the early rain with the latter rain:

> The angel who unites in the proclamation of the third angel's message is to lighten the earth with his glory. A work of worldwide extent and unwonted power is here foretold. ...
>
> The work will be similar to that of the Day of Pentecost. As the "former rain" was given, in the outpouring of the Holy Spirit at the opening of the gospel, to cause the upspringing of the precious seed, so the "latter rain" will be given at its close for the ripening of the harvest. ...
>
> The great work of the gospel is not to close with less manifestation of the power of God than marked its opening. The prophecies

which were fulfilled in the outpouring of the former rain at the opening of the gospel are again to be fulfilled in the latter rain at its close. Here are "the times of refreshing" to which the apostle Peter looked forward.[115]

If the heavenly movement of Christ from the Holy Place to the Most Holy Place in 1844 was accompanied by such a movement on earth that shook the world and began our church, then how much greater will the responsive movement be when Christ's coronation is followed by the great hope of His coming out of the heavenly temple back to this earth? The return of the King does not to happen quietly or in secret. The water and light ceremonies become realities that awaken the earth to the revelation of the King and bring the harvest of the earth to maturity.

His messengers are to prepare the way with a loud cry that awakens the earth to the arrival of her King. The outpouring of the Holy Spirit in the form of His "perfecting latter rain"[116] empowers God's people to proclaim this message. Accompanied by the angel who enlightens the earth with his glory (see Rev. 18:1), we are to go forth and extend the invitation to restoration through the worship of the King to every creature under heaven. "And this gospel of the kingdom [the King] shall be preached in all the world for a witness unto all nations: and then shall the end come" (Matt. 24:14).

> *If the heavenly movement of Christ from the Holy Place to the Most Holy Place in 1844 was accompanied by such a movement on earth that shook the world and began our church, then how much greater will the responsive movement be when Christ's coronation is followed by the great hope of His coming out of the heavenly temple back to this earth?*

The KING is Coming!

---

[115]Ellen G. White, The Great Controversy (Mountain View, CA: Pacific Press Publishing Association), pp. 611, 612
[116]Ellen G. White, Testimonies to Ministers and Gospel Workers (Mountain View, CA: Pacific Press Publishing Association, 1923), p. 508.

"BLESSED BE THE NAME OF GOD FOREVER AND EVER:
FOR WISDOM AND MIGHT ARE HIS:
HE CHANGETH THE TIMES AND THE SEASONS:
HE REMOVETH KINGS AND SETTETH UP KINGS;
HE GIVETH WISDOM UNTO THE WISE, AND
KNOWLEDGE TO THOSE WHO HAVE
UNDERSTANDING:
HE REVEALETH DEEP AND SECRET THINGS:
HE KNOWETH WHAT IS IN THE DARKNESS, AND
LIGHT DWELLETH WITH HIM.

I THANK THEE AND PRAISE THEE, O GOD
OF MY FATHERS,
WHO HAST GIVEN ME WISDOM AND MIGHT,
AND HAST MADE KNOWN UNTO ME
NOW WHAT WE DESIRE OF THEE:
FOR THOU HAST MADE KNOWN TO US"

THE VISIONS OF THE KING
DANIEL 2:20–23

Bibliography

Anderson, Roy Allen. *Unfolding Daniel's Prophecies*. Nampa, ID: Pacific Press Publishing Association, 1975.

Andrews Study Bible, New King James Version. Berrien Springs, MI: Andrews University Press, 2010.

Brown, Raymond. *The New Jerome Biblical Commentary*. Upper Saddle River, NJ: Prentice Hall, 1990.

Engnell, Ivan. *Studies in Divine Kingship in the Ancient Near East*. Oxford: Basil Blackwell, 1967.

Harris, Laird. *Theological Wordbook of the Old Testament*. Chicago: Moody Bible Institute, 1980.

Johnson, Aubrey. *Sacral Kingship in Ancient Israel*. Eugene OR: Wipf & Stock Publishers, 1955.

Schauss, Hayyim. *The Jewish Festivals*. New York: Schoken Books, 1996.

Nichol, F.D. Ed., *The Seventh-day Adventist Bible Commentary*. Vol. 4?. Washington, DC: Review and Herald Publishing Association, 1954.

Smith, Uriah. *Daniel and the Revelation*. Nashville: Southern Publishing Association, 1949.

The Harper Collins Study Bible, New Revised Standard Version. San Francisco: Harper Collins Publishers, 1993.

The Septuagint with Apocrypha: Greek and English. Peabody, MA: Hendrickson Publishers, 1992.

Strong, James. *Strong's Exhaustive Concordance*. Peabody, MA: Hendrickson Publishers, 2007.

White, Ellen G. *The Acts of the Apostles*. Mountain View, CA: Pacific Press Publishing Association, 1911.
White, Ellen G. *The Adventist Home*. Hagerstown, MD: Review and Herald Publishing Association, 1952.
White, Ellen G. "The Closing Work." The Review Herald, October 13, 1904.
White, Ellen G. *Counsels to Parents, Teachers, and Students*. Mountain View, CA: Pacific Press Publishing Association, 1913.
White, Ellen G. *Christ's Object Lessons*. Washington, DC: Review and Herald Publishing Association, 1900.
White, Ellen G. *The Desire of Ages*. Mountain View, CA: Pacific Press Publishing Association, 1898.
White, Ellen G. *Early Writings*. Washington, DC: Review and Herald Publishing Association 1882.
White, Ellen G. *Education*. Mountain View, CA: Pacific Press Publishing Association, 1903.
White, Ellen G. *Gospel Workers*. Washington, DC: Review and Herald Publishing Association, 1915.
White, Ellen G. *The Great Controversy*. Mountain View, CA: Pacific Press Publishing Association, 1911.
White, Ellen G. *Life Sketches of Ellen G. White*. Mountain View, CA: Pacific Press Publishing Association, 1915.
White, Ellen G. *Patriarchs and Prophets*. Washington, DC: Review and Herald Publishing Association, 1890.
White, Ellen G. "The Prayer That God Accepts," *The Review and Herald*, February 9, 1897.
White, Ellen G. *Selected Messages*. Book 2. Washington, DC: Review and Herald Publishing Association, 1958.
White, Ellen G. *Spiritual Gifts*. Vol. 3. Battle Creek, MI: Seventh-day Adventist Publishing Association, Washington D.C. 1864.
White, Ellen G. *The Story of Redemption*. Washington, DC: Review and Herald Publishing Association, 1947.
White, Ellen G. *Testimonies for the Church*. Vol. 1. Mountain View, CA: Pacific Press Publishing Association, 1868.
White, Ellen G. *Testimonies for the Church*. Vol. 2. Mountain View, CA: Pacific Press Publishing Association, 1871.
White, Ellen G. *Testimonies for the Church*. Vol. 5. Mountain View, CA: Pacific Press Publishing Association, 1889.

White, Ellen G. *Testimonies to Ministers and Gospel Workers*. Mountain View, CA: Pacific Press Publishing Association, 1923.

White, Ellen G. *Ye Shall Receive Power*. Hagerstown, MD: Review and Herald Publishing Association, 1995.

TEACH Services, Inc.
P U B L I S H I N G

We invite you to view the complete
selection of titles we publish at:
www.TEACHServices.com

We encourage you to write us
with your thoughts about this,
or any other book we publish at:
info@TEACHServices.com

TEACH Services' titles may be purchased in
bulk quantities for educational, fund-raising,
business, or promotional use.
bulksales@TEACHServices.com

Finally, if you are interested in seeing
your own book in print, please contact us at:
publishing@TEACHServices.com
We are happy to review your manuscript at no charge.

www.ingramcontent.com/pod-product-compliance
Lightning Source LLC
Chambersburg PA
CBHW070554160426
43199CB00014B/2499